How to Organise (and Win!)

CAR TREASURE HUNTS

Researched and written by

Allan Frost

AJF Paperback Originals

By the same author:
The Story of Donnington and its Parish Church (1979)
The Stracyl of Unity (Fantasy novel, 1991)
Priorslee Remembered (1993)
Death and Disaster in Victorian Telford (1996)
Official Handbook to the Myth & Magic Collection (1998)

Notwithstanding the information and suggestions made in this book, neither the author nor the publishers can be held responsible for any consequential loss or damage caused to individuals or property as a result of its contents. It is up to the reader to ensure that common-sense prevails and the laws governing use of the Public Highway and the Motor vehicles (Competitions and Trials) Regulations are adhered to.

ISBN 0 9538085 0 5

British Library Cataloguing in Publication Data:
A catalogue record for this book is available from the British Library.

Published by AJF Paperback Originals
1 Buttermere Drive, Priorslee, Telford,
Shropshire, TF2 9RE, England.

Printed and bound in Great Britain by
TJ International Ltd, Padstow, Cornwall

CONTENTS

With illustrations by
Helen Coventry, Sharon Riley, Jessica Watson
and the author.

For Tim,

with the hope that he discovers his own treasure...

FOREWORD

Car Treasure Hunts are some of the most popular pastimes in Britain, yet because they are essentially localised affairs they rarely get publicised or recognised as important leisure activities. The same is true of Mystery Drives.

They can be the source of great fun, a sporting and intellectual challenge not only for the participants but also for the organisers. Hunts are sometimes described as crosswords on wheels but without the formality of a grid; it is a fair analogy.

A Treasure Hunt requires certain rules and conventions to be observed if the event is not to fail dismally, end in disaster or ruin a reputation.

Each and every clue or instruction must be readily understandable by the hunters. A hunt where only the organiser stands any chance of winning misses the point entirely; there is no pleasure in taking part where the odds are stacked against you before the game begins.

However, like the crossword, clues can be as devious or obscure as it is possible to make them but the participants must have the same chance of being able to decipher them if only to make the hunt more competitive.

Furthermore, the safety and well-being of everyone must be guaranteed as far as possible. Today's roads are often busy and full of potential dangers. The last thing anyone wants is to have an accident whilst having fun. It is the organiser's responsibility to minimise the opportunities for disaster to strike and the competitor's responsibility to look after him (or her) self and the other members of the team.

This book covers matters which must be taken into account when a Car Treasure Hunt is being organised as well as what should and should not be done when taking part in the hunt itself.

Observe everything that is written. As an organiser, you will achieve a reputation for putting on a well organised, fair, safe and enjoyable event. As a contestant, you will increase your chances of winning!

Not everyone will agree with everything written in this book. Some organisers will have their own way of doing things and may consistently organise successful hunts. Others, however, may not be aware of ways in which their events could be improved. Learning and adaptation should be an ongoing process for everyone.

I hope this book will encourage those of you who have hitherto been reluctant to take on the challenge of organising a hunt. It can be more rewarding than winning one organised by someone else!

Allan Frost
Priorslee, Telford

Chapter 1

LEGALITIES

All motoring events, including Car Treasure Hunts, which take place either completely or substantially on the Public Highway, are subject to authorisation by either the Royal Automobile Club Motor Sports Association (MSA) or (for events to be held in Scotland where the Regulations are slightly different) the Royal Scottish Automobile Club (RSAC).

This is not to say that every single event, however small, has to be authorised; there are certain events which do not require formal consent and these are the subject of this handbook.

Even so, it is essential that the prospective Car Treasure Hunt organiser appreciates what does and does not require authorisation in order to avoid an unwitting breach of the Law. The last thing anyone wants is to fall foul of the Police or cause injury to hunt participants or innocent bystanders.

The Motor Vehicles (Competitions and Trials) Regulations 1969 (with subsequent amendments) govern the authorisation of all motoring events which take place on the Public Highway.

The Department of Transport has appointed the Royal Automobile Club Motor Sports Association (MSA) as the Controlling Agency in England and Wales. The MSA's Competition Authorisation Section (CAS) handles all the relevant legislation and issues guidelines to event organisers as well as granting authorisations. The RSAC (Motor Sports) Limited (RSACMS) performs similar duties for events held in Scotland.

The Regulations require that all events, apart from the exceptions noted in this handbook, are authorised by the CAS. Applications for events for which authorisation is required must be submitted not more than six months and not less than two months before the event is to take place. Specified major events are excluded from this time limit and are well outside the scope of this book.

The CAS is only permitted to issue authority for a certain number of events on any road in any particular period, so, if you think authorisation is required for an event you are organising, it is important that applications are submitted as early as possible to avoid the disappointment of permission being refused. At best the CAS may be able to offer an alternative date or suggest an alternative route but this cannot be guaranteed. There may also be restrictions, subject to localised tolerance levels and conditions, which can vary from area to area.

The MSA Yearbook contains full details of its regulations and requirements and is available from them upon payment. Unless you are involved in Motor Club activities and run regular events for which authorisation is required, purchase of the Yearbook may not be relevant. Nevertheless, it is a book well worth acquiring if you are a serious Car Treasure Hunter.

The Control of Motor Rallies legislation takes into account the recommendations of an Advisory Committee whose findings were agreed by the Government. One of the Committee's recommendations was that the cost of the authorisation procedures should not be borne by the general taxpayer.

Consequently, the MSA (or, in Scotland, the RSACMS) must levy a charge for all events which require their authorisation. There is a scale of fees payable which depends upon a number of variables; for example, the distance of the event and the number of vehicles taking part. The MSA (or RSACMS) will provide full details upon request, including an application form together with advisory notes. These notes are useful to *everyone* involved in organising Car Treasure Hunts.

If you are in any doubt whatsoever about an event you are organising, contact the MSA (or RSACMS) at the earliest opportunity for advice.

Authorisation Contacts

Royal Automobile Club Motor Sports Association Limited
Motor Sports House, Riverside Park, Colnbrook, Slough, SL3 0HG, England.
Telephone 01753 - 681736.
e-mail: msa_mail@compuserve.com

Royal Scottish Automobile Club (Motor Sports) Limited
11 Blythswood Square, Glasgow, G2 4AG, Scotland.
Telephone 0141 - 204 - 4999.
e-mail: rsac_motorsport@compuserve.com

Now read on. . . the rest of this book is for ordinary folk who want to organise or take part in Car Treasure Hunts without the need to get entangled with the intricacies of formal authorisation!

The Thrill of the Chase!

Chapter 2

TYPES OF TREASURE HUNT

This chapter deals with the criteria which should be observed if you wish to organise a Car Treasure Hunt without having to suffer the inconvenience of seeking formal authorisation. Organising (and taking part in) the two main types of event, the **Standard Treasure Hunt** and the **Navigational Scatter Event,** are the subjects of the remainder of this handbook. The **Mystery Drive,** a variation on the Standard Treasure Hunt, is also covered.

In spite of what has been written in Chapter One, there are several types of Car Treasure Hunt which do not require authorisation since they are automatically approved under the terms of The Motor Vehicles (Competitions and Trials) Regulations; these are the events much loved by sports and social clubs, societies, families and friends and provide an enjoyable challenge to all who participate.

If you intend to organise a Car Treasure Hunt, these are the types of event to organise. Providing that you stick to the following guidelines, there is no need to seek authorisation from the MSA (or RSACMS).

Mystery Drives

These are, to all intents and purposes, governed by the same rules as Standard Treasure Hunts which are detailed below.

The main difference is that the clues are little more than directions to be followed in order to reach a particular destination.

This type of hunt is ideal for competitors who simply want to have a brief journey into the countryside and to meet up with friends or family at a popular or pretty venue.

Standard Treasure Hunt

This is the most popular type of hunt and guidelines are:

- No more than twelve competitors' cars are allowed to take part. The organiser's car is not counted, provided that no one in the car is a competitor.
- Within an eight-day period, no part of the event takes place on another route organised by the same promoter (organiser), whether or not it is for the same club or group of people, or where the organisers of both events are members of the same club.

In other words, you may organise a hunt with a maximum of twelve cars taking part but you aren't allowed to hold another event (for the same or different competitors) which traverses the same route, either in whole or in part, unless a clear eight days have elapsed between events.

- No time or mileage restrictions should be placed on completing the event (although a finishing time may be specified as long as it gives adequate time to visit the required number of places).
- There should be a set route.
- Competitors do not necessarily have to vacate their cars to find the answers to clues.

Twelve cars may not seem very many but, when you consider that each car may hold four team members, 48 people could participate. Furthermore, twelve answer sheets is more than enough to check at the finishing post!

Standard Treasure Hunts follow a specified route which may be littered with clues, one clue leading to the next. The starting and finishing points are the same for everyone taking part and each car's members form a team.

Each team is in competition to see if they can a) follow the correct route and b) solve the most clues. Although this may sound simple, it is surprising how much confusion and disagreement can arise during the couple of hours it takes to complete the course.

An important point to bear in mind is that cars participating in this type of hunt may average only about ten to fifteen miles per hour. The length of the hunt is, however, up to the organiser, but should rarely exceed 30 to 35 miles.

Where possible, aim for a duration of about two hours – any more and concentration begins to flag, tempers get frayed (especially if it rains) and the event will not be so enjoyable. It is often better to have a short route with an abundance of clues.

There must be no time limit set on completing the course; to do so could encourage competitors to break speed limits. Always allow sufficient time for the last car embarking on the hunt to reach the end of the course before closing time and/or before last meals are served at the destination.

Car Treasure Hunts of this type with more than twelve cars competing require formal authorisation; this inevitably adds to the cost of running the event as well as causing more work for the organiser. So, unless you have absolutely no option, keep the number of cars to twelve or less.

Navigational Scatter Event

This type of hunt has no set route but, in order to qualify for automatic authorisation, it is essential that these conditions are observed:

- No more than twelve cars may take part. The organiser's car is not counted, provided that no one in the car is a competitor.
- No time or mileage restrictions should be placed on completing the event (although a finishing time may be specified as long as it gives adequate time to visit the required number of places).
- There should be no set route.
- Places to be visited must be detailed to the competitors in no fixed order (not like in the Standard Treasure Hunt where one clue location leads logically on to the next).
- Competitors must be free to choose which of the places they visit and not be required to visit more than 75% of the places detailed. So, if the hunt consists of a possible twelve locations, no competing car should be required to visit more than nine of them (i.e. 75% of the total).
- Competitors must be required to vacate their cars to reach the points where clues are to be found. This

means that the cars are to be used as a form of transport to arrive at a particular place but that the clue appropriate to that place is to be found away from where the cars are likely to be parked.

This type of hunt may consist of up to twelve encrypted places to visit; the name of each location is provided in the form of a clue. Competitors should be required to visit (and hence discover the answers to the clues for no more than) nine of the twelve locations.

Each place to be visited also has a clue for something to be found which is only appropriate to that particular location and (hopefully) not to any of the other places included in the hunt.

For most competitions of this type, it is best if each place to be visited is no more than about five miles away (as the crow flies) from any one of the other locations.

Because teams may be unable to decipher the name of some of the places it follows that there can be no set or predetermined route which all the cars must follow.

In this type of hunt, the clues for the places to visit are usually quite difficult to solve, while the answer to the clue to be discovered in each place is relatively straightforward.

If you are in any doubt about whether your event fits all these requirements, contact the MSA (or RSACMS).

Road Safety Event

These are events designed to concentrate on and assess each driver's behaviour, paying particular attention to good performance and compliance with the Highway Code. They may take place either partially or wholly on the Public Highway.

Organisers of such events may well be members of driving or motoring clubs and may not necessarily regard them as Treasure Hunts.

Provided less than twelve cars take part and there are no time or minimum mileage limits imposed, there is no need to seek authorisation.

Because of the specialised nature of Road Safety Events, they are outside the scope of this handbook.

Armed Forces Event

This is an event in which each and every participant is a member of the British Armed Forces and the event itself is designed solely for their Service training.

This type of event is well outside the scope of this handbook, although the Armed Services may find the contents useful...

and finally... Penalties

The Police may prosecute and the Courts may impose financial penalties on anyone promoting or taking part in an unauthorised competition on the Public Highway.

It is recommended that, whenever you begin to organise a hunt for your colleagues, associates, friends or family, you check with the MSA (or RSACMS) to ensure that there have been no changes to the Regulations as stated in this handbook.

Both organisations will be pleased to offer advice, including whether the Police should be informed of your event.

Directional instructions must be made clear!

Chapter 3

WHICH HUNT TO CHOOSE?

From now on, this handbook takes it for granted that no more than twelve cars will participate and that the guidelines stated in Chapter Two relating to the type of hunt chosen are being followed. Deciding which type of hunt to organise is the first problem the organiser has to consider. By restricting the number of cars, the organiser can concentrate on the business of organising the event without the additional inconvenience of having to submit detailed proposals required by the authorising body.

The basic requirements of the three main types of hunt are the subject of this chapter. Prospective organisers will be able to decide which is appropriate for the event they wish to prepare. Subsequent chapters go into much greater detail to ensure that comprehensive guidance is given to take the organisation through the various stages of preparation. Always bear in mind that safety and the enjoyment of everyone involved are the primary concerns.

The simplest event to organise is the **Mystery Drive,** which mainly requires the preparation of (fairly) detailed instructions on how to get from a common starting point for all competitors to a single destination.

Because there is no need to look out for a large number of roadside clues (as required in Standard Treasure Hunts), this type of event is ideal where the intention is purely to guide participants along an interesting or pretty route through the countryside to a pleasant destination.

As such, Mystery Drives are very popular with small groups (such as church organisations and families) where relative harmony between each car's occupants is desirable. If the journey's instructions are clear, there should be no argument or tension and an enjoyable time can be had looking at the sights and scenery.

It is common for Mystery Drives to end at a country pub, family tourist attraction, clubhouse or church hall where refreshments can be served to the competitors. Because there are no answer sheets to be marked, the organiser need only be concerned with the accuracy of his (or her) instructions together with the catering facilities at the final venue.

Variations to the format can, of course, be made. The Mystery Drive may take the form of two destinations instead of a single one: when the event begins, each participating car is given instructions on how to reach the first destination, where light refreshments (a drink or ice cream) may be obtained and a second sheet containing instructions to reach the second (final) venue can be handed out. It is at the final venue that competitors receive a well-earned rest together with more substantial refreshment.

Depending on how much extra responsibility the organiser wants or is willing to undertake, a sheet of general knowledge questions could also be handed to each car for completion by the occupants while they are travelling. No more than about twenty questions is adequate – the objective is to provide a little extra amusement, not detract from the scenic drive!

If a quiz is provided and the event is a double-destination one, competitors should be required to hand in their answer sheets when they reach the first venue. This should give the organiser plenty of time to mark them and announce the results by the time everyone has reached the final destination.

It is customary to award prizes whenever a quiz is held. The cost of these should be covered by asking all participants to pay a modest entry fee. The entry fee should also take into account any collective costs involved in hiring a room at the destination(s) as well as refreshments.

It is strongly suggested that entry fees are collected before the event in case someone backs out and leaves the organiser with an unexpected personal expense!

Obviously, it is easier for the organiser to book a venue where no charge is imposed (and where competitors buy their own refreshments on arrival) and not to organise a quiz. However, having everything paid for before the event means less inconvenience and encourages participants to turn up! Furthermore, a short quiz provides a little more enjoyment to the occasion.

Both the Standard Treasure Hunt and Navigational Scatter Event require a great deal more planning. Of the two, the **Standard Treasure Hunt** is more demanding to organise because there are many questions to devise and a set route has to be decided.

The organisation of Standard Treasure Hunts requires patience, an eye for detail, negotiation skills – and more! Whilst they are not to be undertaken lightly, a successful hunt can result in a great sense of achievement for the organiser as well as the competitors.

There is an awful lot to consider but, taken one step at a time, everything will fall into place and should not be beyond most people's capabilities once they set their mind to the task in hand. To summarise,

- A venue must be chosen and arrangements made for the comfort of all participants and their vehicles, suitable refreshment and other essential facilities, including toilets.
- A fixed route is essential; there must be no deviation so it is important that directions are given clearly.
- A substantial quantity of clues of varying difficulty have to be devised.
- The event must be advertised.
- Entrance fees (to cover the cost of prizes, meals and, if necessary, the expenses incurred by the organiser in presenting the event).
- Simple accounts should be kept to record all income and expenditure associated with the event.
- Relevant stationery (entrance tickets, question sheets, posters, etc.) must be prepared and checked thoroughly.
- The nature of prizes considered and then purchased.

- A car (with someone else to drive it while the organiser takes notes) is essential. The route will need to be traversed several times before the event takes place.
- The organiser must maintain control over competitors during the event and afterwards at the chosen venue.
- It may be necessary to liaise with official bodies (e.g. the Police, landowners, residents, caterers, landlords, etc.).
- Secrecy must be maintained so that none of the competitors has any idea of your plans.
- A lot of time will need to be spent on preparation.

The amount of work involved should not be underestimated; preparation is the key to a successful event. Organising your first event will, if you are conscientious and want it to succeed, probably cause sleepless nights and some friction between yourself and colleagues, family and friends when your obsession takes over your life (or, at least, seems to!).

The second and subsequent events will be so much easier to prepare; at least you'll have a better idea of what is involved.

The criteria for a **Navigational Scatter Event** (Scatter Event or Hunt) are similar to those for the Standard Treasure Hunt except that there is no set route or anywhere near the number of clues. Consequently they take less time to organise.

If you still can't decide which format to chose, read the detailed notes in the next few chapters.

Chapter 4

TOOLS FOR THE JOB

Irrespective of the type of hunt you choose to prepare, it is important that you assemble the basic tools to enable you to do the job effectively. This chapter details the items you are most likely to need.

Basic tools:

- An A4-size pad of lined paper together with a clip-board, pen and pencil. You'll need these to make notes.
- A coloured highlighter pen may also be useful to draw attention to important notes.
- A ring binder with a supply of plastic wallets which fit inside. The binder keeps all your notes in one place where they can be easily found. The wallets can be used to keep related items together.
- A watch to keep a note of approximate times. Although you must not set a time limit, it's important to have some idea how long the hunt may take.
- Map(s) of the area covered by the proposed route. Those in the Landranger Series produced by the Ordnance Survey are probably best as they are fairly large scale and show a lot of detail.
- A computer and printer or, at the very least, a type-writer for preparing all the stationery, especially the clue sheets. A computer with a word processor or page-lay-out ('publishing') program makes it much easier and quicker to produce and amend the paperwork. If you don't have access to a computer, then a photocopier will be necessary to reproduce the clue sheets in the quantity required.

- A supply of good quality paper and card to produce the clue sheets, tickets, posters, etc. as well as some envelopes (for the Panic instructions – more of that later).
- A small cash book for noting income and expenditure relating to the hunt as well as a cash box to keep the entry fees safe.
- A copy of the current Highway Code (available from book shops and some newsagents) in case you need to check on anything relating to activities on the Public Highway.
- A variety of reference books (including this one!) such as those listed in the appendices.
- A telephone for making arrangements and a manned telephone in case of emergencies when the hunt is taking place.
- A car, preferably with a trip clock measuring tenths of a mile which will enable you to check distances. The car should be insured for leisure activities such as Treasure Hunts: check with your insurers if you're not sure.
- An accomplice to help by driving the car as you travel the potential route in search of clues and to help with incidental matters. This must be someone whom you can trust, will put up with your impatience and be willing and able to help.
- Competitors. Without them, the hunt will not take place. Presumably you have someone in mind...

Useful additions:

- A camera in case you want to include photographs of places or things to find as part of the hunt. It will also be required if you want to take photographs of competitors during the hunt itself (as a record of the event). A video camera (or camcorder) could also be used to record the event.

- A scanner fitted to a computer will enable you to include photographs and drawings on the clue sheets.
- A hand-held compass in case you need to indicate a direction either in the travel instructions or where to look to find the answer to a clue.
- Plastic bags (for competitors to collect any items of 'treasure' you specify as part of the hunt).
- A torch and umbrella in case you get lost at night in the rain!

These lists are by no means fully comprehensive. Organisers should to add to them in the light of experience.

Do Not Trespass!

Chapter 5

MYSTERY DRIVES: CONSIDERATIONS

Perhaps the most important considerations when organising a Mystery Dive are the following:

- **Who will be taking part?**

Will they be people in a particular age group? Are they members (and partners) of an organisation? Do any of them have special needs, e.g. disabled, elderly or young? If so, what are they?

You will probably know what sort of folk are likely to take part but you may have to consider certain restrictions. For example, the drive you have in mind may not be suitable for children. On the other hand, you may want it to be specifically for families or a group of elderly or disabled citizens.

Something to bear in mind at this point is that each car taking part will form, to all intents and purposes, a team. This being the case, will each car be able to accommodate the likely composition of each team? If the drive is for individual families, the chances are that each family will be able to fit into one (their own) vehicle.

However, if the participants are from almost any other group (such as an office or organisation) it will be necessary for you to consider getting involved in allocating individuals to make up the quantity to fill each car. Most cars can comfortably seat (and be insured for) a maximum of four people (including the driver) but some may take more and others less.

You must remember that twelve cars (excluding your own, providing it contains no competitors) is the limit, so some juggling may be necessary to make sure as many people as want to take part can do so without any laws being broken or insurance being invalidated.

- **Where are the participants are likely to start the journey?**

Will it be someone's house (perhaps the organiser's)? Or the car park belonging to a church, public house, club, school, office, etc.? Or somewhere else?

Bear in mind that thirteen cars (twelve competitors' plus your own) take up a fair amount of space. Even though you may specify staggered times for each of the vehicles to meet at the starting point, some will probably arrive earlier than expected. Furthermore, you will need to spend a few minutes talking to the team in each car just before they depart to make sure they understand your instructions.

This being the case, consider whether or not you will need to obtain permission from the car park owner before proceeding. If the car park belongs to the organisation for which the event is intended, probably not. On the other hand, if the event will start at a public house or other private car park, it is imperative that you obtain permission (preferably in writing) from the landlord or owner.

- **Where would you like the final destination to be?**

Will it be a church hall, public house, club, beauty spot, theme park, etc.? Will it be back at the starting point? If so, should this be a double-destination event, with the first venue situated somewhere near the furthest point of the journey? Will light refreshments and facilities be available at the first venue?

The final destination should not be too far away from the homes of most of the participants: they will not welcome a long drive back afterwards at a time when they are likely to be tired and less alert.

- **How long do you want the overall event to take?**

Bear in mind that not everyone will start at the same time (it's not a race!). Not everyone drives at the same speed, especially if some want to stop the car for a few minutes to enjoy the view or to take a comfort break.

The actual time spent travelling will depend very much on the sort of group for whom you are catering. Children, the disabled and elderly may find a journey of more than an hour without a break uncomfortable.

That is why a double-destination event may have its attractions. Others will be quite happy to go for a couple of hours without a break.

What sort of roads do you intend to travel? Are they busy, fast, slow, likely to suffer from traffic congestion, especially at weekends or Bank holidays? Major or minor roads? Even motorways?

Will the event take place during the evening (in which case a shorter period of time will be available, not just for the journey but also at the destination) or at the weekend or during daytime (which gives scope for a longer journey and more time to be spent at the final venue)?

- **What do you intend to happen at the final destination?**

Will refreshments be provided, such as a bar meal, or will everyone be expected to bring their own picnic? If a bar meal and it is a probable requirement, will vegetarians be catered for? What are the facilities (e.g. toilets, parking, disabled access)? Will participants go on a country walk or a visit to a monument? Will they be expected to take part in a sporting activity, such as a game of Rounders?

With this type of drive, it is essential to have a purpose for the event because the actual journey should be fairly straightforward.

Many people will enjoy a convivial time chatting with friends and having a meal. Others may want to explore the surroundings or take part in a more demanding activity, such as a fun game or a General Knowledge quiz.

In any event, refreshments and essential facilities must be readily available at the destination.

If the objective is to pursue some other activity, will you be expected to organise it (not within the scope of this handbook!) or will someone else be able to take care of that side of the proceedings? If so, liaise with them closely.

- **Will you need to impose an entry fee?**

Will there be prizes awarded at the final destination? If so, what will they be – store tokens, bottles of wine or spirits, a trophy, certificates, or what? How many will there be; first, second and third prizes? Will there be a single prize for each winning team or separate prizes for each winning team's members? Will you need to recover the cost of presenting the event? Will car drivers expect to be reimbursed for their petrol?

- **Will the cost of refreshments be fixed for each participant?**

If so, it will be easier to include the cost as part of the entry fee: that way you can settle the bill quickly rather than have to wait for each person to order and pay for their own food separately. If not, it might be better if each person orders and pays for themselves.

It is important that you cover your overall personal costs and make sure everyone who is required to pay does so before the event takes place. You may need to check each participant's personal preferences when it comes to ordering food, in which case try to obtain a menu from the venue and order the meals (and even pay for them) beforehand.

You will need to emphasise that deposits are not refundable unless someone else is able to substitute.

When you have answered these questions and have a clear idea of what the purpose of the Mystery Drive will be, you are ready to begin planning the event.

Chapter 6

MYSTERY DRIVES: PLANNING

First Venue

The sorts of things to check at a destination depend very much on what you hope to accomplish.

If it is the first venue in a double-destination event you should make sure that there are:

- A car park suitable for the number of cars in your event as well as those belonging to anyone else who might happen to be there on the day and at the time you expect your competitors to be present.
- Toilets (including facilities for anyone with special needs who may take part).
- Light refreshments (drinks, ice creams, etc.)
- Any other required or desirable facilities, e.g. protection from inclement weather.

Check to see if there are any other aspects to be taken into account, such as parking fees, admission charges, etc. If so, what are the costs involved? They will need to be accounted for and usually included in the entry fee payable by everyone taking part in the event.

Also check on the approximate prices of the refreshments so that you can give some idea of what they are in case your participants ask and (most important) will the venue be open at the proposed day and time of the event?

Finally, check with the owner, landlord, etc. (if there is one) to make sure that there are no objections to your group using the venue.

Get the name and telephone number in case you need to discuss things at a later date (you might want to discuss group discounts, if nothing else).

Most places serving the public are quite happy to assist

(after all, they stand to gain) and may offer the use of a private room or to reserve parking spaces. However, there may be objections. If you can't resolve them you'll have to think of an alternative venue.

Write down all the relevant information you discover about the venue at the time you glean it: you can guarantee you'll forget something vital if you try to rely on your memory!

Final Venue

The final destination has to provide the main reason for the Mystery Drive. All the aspects listed for a first venue (even if there isn't one!) must be considered but special attention needs to be paid to the nature of refreshments and the available facilities.

Participants usually expect to be fed, watered and entertained in a place conducive to enjoyment. Watering should be simple enough.

Whilst you can expect everyone to pay for their own drinks without quibbling, providing food is a different matter (unless everyone brings their own picnic).

You will need to find out what choice of food is available together with costs. Try to obtain a menu, ask whether it is necessary to make a reservation and whether orders for all meals should be made in advance.

Better still, try to hire a private room (if it's that sort of establishment); it will help to reduce the likelihood of your group competing with other patrons for service and, if you intend holding a quiz or similar indoor activity, maintain exclusivity and minimise inconvenience.

If the final venue is a national monument, historic building, theme park, etc., ascertain the cost of admission (and parking, if this is separate) and remember to include the admission charges as part of the entry fee for your event. Try to negotiate a reduction in the admission charge if you are making a group booking.

If you intend putting on an outdoor activity (such as a walk or team game), make sure the venue is appropriate and that it is possible to have back-up undercover or indoor entertainment in case weather conditions disrupt your plans. You may need to discuss this with the management at the venue.

The Route

When you have a clear idea of where you want the Mystery Drive to end, think about how you want the cars to get there.

Rather than simply tell participants where the destination is (which somewhat defeats the whole point of a Mystery Drive), think about any interesting places or viewpoints en route.

One of the objectives of the event should be to take your guests along pleasant roads and to drive in a leisurely fashion. Try to avoid motorways and other busy roads. This is where an Ordnance Survey (or similar) map will come in useful.

The only way you can be sure the route is suitable is to travel it yourself. It is better and safer if you can get someone else to do the driving while you make detailed notes on the way. Before setting off, warn the driver that you may want him (or her) to stop at a moment's notice and not to treat the course as a race.

- Start at the place where the actual event will begin.
- Make a note of the mileage or set the trip clock.
- Make sure you have a clipboard, plenty of paper and a couple of pens or pencils.
- And the map(s) covering the route.
- And plenty of petrol in the tank.
- Make a note of the time you set off.

Start making notes as soon as you begin. There are four main aspects to which you should pay particular attention:

- the safety of your prospective travellers,
- the precision of your directions and
- landmarks to ensure your travellers know they are on the right road at all times.
- Do not overtly mention the names of villages or

towns which appear on signposts. The point should be that folk don't know where they're going until they get there!

While you travel the route, keep your eyes open for noticeable features; obvious ones are public houses, where a straightforward clue could be given as to the name of the establishment. For example, if the road passes a pub called The Royal Oak you could call it *The Regal Tree* or *Charles' Hiding Place.* Similarly, Little Chef is often referred to as *Small Cook.*

The important thing to remember is that such clues must be very simple; severe problem solving is not the point behind Mystery Drives, although a little brain-teasing adds an element of fun to the occasion, especially where children are concerned.

An added advantage of passing public-access buildings is that they frequently have facilities (like toilets), which may be useful to mention in your instructions. Check on their days and times of opening!

It helps if fairly precise mileages between recognisable places are stated occasionally. For example, *About three miles after passing The Regal Tree you will see a telephone box on the right.*

Similarly, changes of road or direction must be very clearly indicated.

Instead of saying, *Turn next right* say, *Turn right one mile after passing Hemlock Farm.*

Try to relate the change of direction to an unmissable feature. However, an exception to this general rule might be to *Turn right at the next T junction,* in effect a situation where the current road comes to an end.

Something else to consider is adding snippets of interesting information relating to places en route. To do this may require some local knowledge or a little research. An example could be stated in your instructions as: *In two miles you will see a gibbet on the left by the crossroads. Continue straight on and as you do so ponder on the fact that Bill Breadnicker was the last man to be left hanging about here, in 1723 when he was caught lifting a bag of flour; presumably it wasn't self-raising!* (Humour helps but is not essential!)

Similarly, you may want to invite your travellers to stop at convenient locations to look at something of interest. It could be a view, an historic building or an unusual feature. If you decide to do this, make sure the stopping points are good from a road safety point of view. Say exactly where it is (as part of your itinerary), what's so special about it and approximately how long should be spent there before continuing the journey. Avoid inviting folk to look around a Stately Home: it takes too long. (On the other hand, there is no reason why such a place should not be the final destination.)

By the time you have reached your destination, you should have detailed but straightforward notes that will enable you to break the overall journey down into stages.

Don't worry if you haven't been able to think up alternative names for prominent landmarks; provided you have listed them as part of the itinerary you can ponder over them at a later stage. The same applies to inserting historical information: a brief trip to a local library or book shop will help to fill in gaps and provide some enlightenment both to yourself as well as your guests.

When you stop the car at the destination, make a note of the final mileage as well as the finishing time. If the route seems to be satisfactory and you have not needed to take any detours, you will know how long (in terms of distance) the journey is. Depending on how much time you have spent stopping on the way, you will also have a rough idea of how long (in terms of time) the overall trip is likely to take.

If your Mystery Drive is a double-destination event (where the final venue is at or near the point of original departure), you should consider taking a different route for the return journey; it helps to maintain interest.

You may need to prepare Stage Two instructions following the same procedures as for the outward journey. If the event has only one destination you could provide instructions on how to return to the original departure point by a shorter or quicker route or leave competitors to find their own way back. Use your discretion.

If the length and time of the completed Mystery Drive are acceptable, then this part of the preparation is over.

If they are not, you must reconsider the route and/or the venue and repeat the process until you are happy.

Paperwork

To ensure that your event runs smoothly, some paperwork is inevitable.

This section deals with the most common stationery considerations when running a Mystery Drive.

Not only will they help to keep planning under control but will also give the impression of professionalism to those taking part. Examples of some of the more important items are given for you to adapt according to your own needs.

- **Letters to venues**

It may be necessary for you to write formally to the owners of the venue(s) to obtain confirmation that they are willing to accommodate you and your guests.

- Make sure you present a business-like approach and include everything you deem important to the success of the enterprise. Use headed paper if you are acting on behalf of an organisation. Keep copies of all correspondence.

- **Posters**

Unless you are able to convey details orally to all concerned, you may want to produce a number of posters to advertise the event. Posters should be eye catching and state:

- the type of event (*Mystery Drive and Country Walk, Mystery Drive and Fun Rounders Match, Mystery Drive and Picnic,* etc.)
- the date of the event
- the time it will start and where from

- the expected finishing time if known
- whether refreshments are available and, if so, that the cost is or is not included in the entry fee
- the entry fee and contact name(s) from whom tickets may be obtained
- a general note about what will take place at the final venue (without giving the game away) if this is not implied in the title of the poster.
- If there will be prizes awarded at the end of the event, say so.

- **Participants List**

Prepare a chart to show this information:

- the car number (1 to 12 maximum)
- the occupants of each car (by convention naming the driver first even if someone else is the team leader). This chart will be a useful tool for allocating people to each car to ensure optimum use of the restricted number of vehicles permitted.
- spaces to record the starting time allocated to each car and to record payment of the entry fee for each person (if appropriate).
- The chart could be developed further to include information to be entered on the day of the drive, such as each participating car's registration number and a space against each one to tick when it leaves the starting point and cross-tick when it arrives at the interim or final destination. This additional information will help you check that every-one arrives safely.

- **Tickets**

Prepare tickets (in sufficient quantity to meet your requirements) as shown in the example. Include:

- the name of the organiser or organisation
- the title of the event
- the date of the event

Allan & Co's

Car number

MYSTERY DRIVE & ROUNDERS MATCH

25th May 2000

Departing from: ....

Please ensure you arrive before: ....

Entry fee: £7.50 (to include Bar Meal)

MYSTERY DRIVE PARTICIPANTS LIST

Date of the Event: ....

First arrival time: ....

Last arrival time: ....

Car Number	Team Members	Entry Fees paid in full (✓)	Car to arrive at (time)	Car Reg. No.	Started Drive (✓)	Ended Drive (✓)
1						
2						
3						
4						
5						
6						
7						
8						
9						
10						
11						
12						

- the car number
- the starting point
- the time that car must arrive there and
- the entry fee (plus, perhaps, what is included in the fee, e.g. admittance to the final venue, meal, etc.).

You may also add other notes if there is space, such as the time when the overall event is likely to finish.

The next types of stationery to consider are items required for the event itself. Some of these suggestions are essential; others are optional and depend on what you hope to achieve.

- **Itinerary sheet(s)**

Prepare at least one for each car, plus a few spares.

- Show the organiser's or organisation's name and the title and date of the event at the top of all pages and number them in sequence.
- Then give the general rules of the event and state that it is not a race, that the Highway Code must be observed at all times and that the organiser cannot be held responsible for any loss or damage suffered to participants or property during the event.
- Break the journey up into short numbered stages, remembering to add approximate mileages, interesting information, etc.
- Say what everyone should do when reaching the venue(s) at the end of the journey notes, including *Wait for the organiser,* who will probably arrive after most of the others.
- Include a note to open the Panic Envelope if the car gets lost on the way. Even with the clearest instructions possible, someone is bound to misunderstand or misread them.
- If the event has a double destination, prepare a separate itinerary sheet for both stages and include a note at the end of the instructions for the first

Allan & Co's

MYSTERY DRIVE

25th May 2000

EVERYONE IN THE CAR SHOULD READ THESE NOTES BEFORE SETTING OFF

The Drive is not a race but a leisurely drive through the countryside which should take about 80 minutes (depending on how long you stop at the points mentioned en route). By following the instructions given here you will eventually arrive at the destination where refreshments await you. If your car has one, it may help if you zero the trip clock now; otherwise make a note of your starting mileage here: ....

Your car should be roadworthy and the Highway Code must be observed at all times. Valid driving licences and insurance cover must exist for everyone who drives during the Drive. The safety of all team members rests with the driver/owner of each car; the organiser cannot be held responsible for loss or damage to persons or property sustained whilst the Drive is in progress.

Particular care should be taken when stopping the car to ensure no obstruction is caused to other road users. Similarly, take care when leaving the car, even on the quieter stretches. Always check that there is nothing coming which could harm yourself or other road users.

If you are nowhere near finishing by _____ o'clock or if there is an emergency and you need to seek help urgently, open the Panic Envelope. The contents will tell you where the Drive ends and give you an emergency telephone number.

Please take a few moments to familiarise yourself with the instructions before setting off on your Drive. If you need further clarification, ask the organiser now. Once you set off, you're on your own!

When you arrive at the destination, stop at the far end of the car park. There are toilets in the first building. We shall be waiting for you in the private room of the second building.

Good luck – and have a safe journey.

DIRECTIONS

1. Leave the car park and turn left. Continue along the road until you come to a T junction, where you turn right. About 2 miles along this road you will see The Romantic Flower and Monarch's Headpiece (where the diarist Samuel Pepys spent many happy hours writing 'and so to bed...') on the left. Take the third turning on the left after seeing this building.

2. You should now have travelled about 8 miles. Drive along this narrow road for almost 3 miles when you will see a blue P layby on the left at the top of a hill. Stop in the layby and get out of the car for about 5 minutes. If you look through the gateway into the field you will see the remains of an ancient abbey far to the right, whilst to the left you can see the ruins of a convent. Both establishments were dissolved by Henry VIII in 1538. Rumour has it that there is a secret tunnel connecting the two buildings...

3. Get back into the car and continue on your way. After two miles you will pass through a pretty village and its ford. Notice the remarkable shrine-like spring some 100 metres on the right after the ford. After about three more miles you will arrive at a crossroads; drive straight over and continue past a rather smelly pig farm on the left. This is where they rear the little piggies for the Monday market although most would prefer to stay at home...

Continued on Page 2...

stage advising participants that they should collect the second stage instructions from the organiser when they reach the first destination.

• If you want to include a quiz as part of the first stage of the event, mention it in the instructions and say that the answer sheets must be handed to the organiser when the first venue is reached and will be marked in time for when everyone arrives at the final destination.

• If you are giving each car a notice (see below) to put in their front or rear window, ask for it to be displayed at all times when the event is in progress. Mention that the card must not obstruct the driver's view.

- **Panic Envelopes**

Prepare one Panic Envelope (sealed and clearly marked) for each vehicle taking part. It should contain:

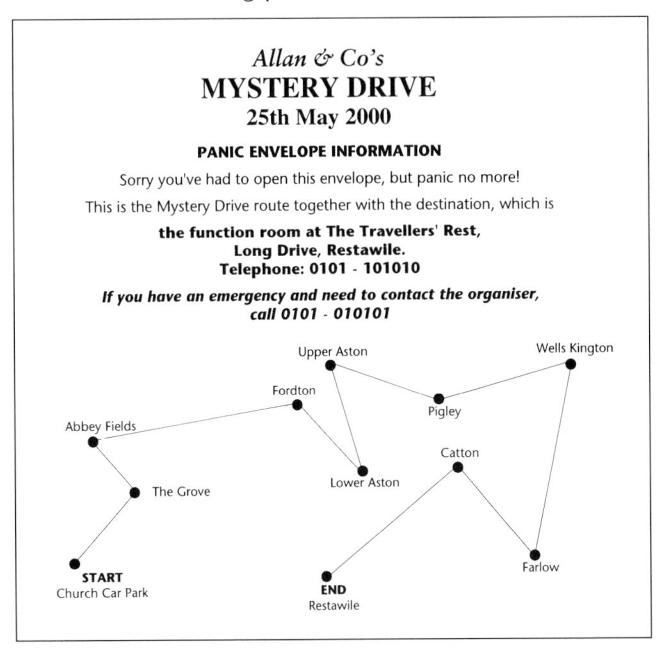
Allan & Co's

MYSTERY DRIVE

25th May 2000

PANIC ENVELOPE INFORMATION

Sorry you've had to open this envelope, but panic no more!

This is the Mystery Drive route together with the destination, which is

the function room at The Travellers' Rest,
Long Drive, Restawile.
Telephone: 0101 - 101010

If you have an emergency and need to contact the organiser, call 0101 - 010101

- the exact name and location of the final venue
- a simplified map of the overall route (including all of stage one and stage two with both venues clearly identified). Although it might be easier to photocopy part of an Ordnance Survey or similar map and highlight the route in coloured ink, this may constitute a breach of copyright unless you obtain prior permission (possibly involving payment of a fee) from the map's creator.
- a (manned) telephone number in case of emergency. Ideally, this would be the organiser's mobile telephone number (if he has one). Otherwise, give the number of a reliable person who is not taking part in the event and does not mind taking responsibility in an emergency should the situation arise.

- **Car Notices**

You might wish to ask each car to display a small card notice in their front or rear window so that participants can identify each other on the road. Such notices are also an easy way to identify participants if the venue car park has spaces allocated to your party.

Car notices are best produced cheaply with black print on a bright yellow card. Each card (maximum size A4) should show the organiser's or organisation's name and the car number (1 to 12 and O for the organiser's car).

Other Paperwork

Depending on your plans, other items of paperwork may constitute:

- **Quiz Question Sheets,** preferably with all questions on a single side of paper. Produce one for each car.
  - Show the organiser's or organisation's name and the title and date of the quiz at the top of the sheet.
  - Then have a line or box in which to write the team's car number.
  - Number each question on the left and put a line or box to the right for the answers to be entered.

Allan & Co's
MYSTERY DRIVE QUIZ
25th May 2000

Car Number

While you are driving along, try to answer these questions. Only one answer should be given to each question; multiple answers will be disregarded even if one happens to be correct. Please write the answers in ink and do not write in the 'Marks' column.

Hand your completed sheet to the organiser when you reach the venue at the end of Stage One of the Mystery Drive.

Question Number	Question	Answer	Marks
1	Who was the cabin boy in 'Treasure Island'?		
2	Who sang the title song for the James Bond film 'Diamonds are Forever'?		
3	In which year did the Great Train Robbery occur?		
4	Which American State is called the 'Silver State'?		
5	What is the name of the ram's coat sought after by the Argonauts?		
6	What bodily feature may show 'silver threads among the gold'?		
7	If you were born into wealth, what sort of cutlery might you have in your mouth?		
8	Which Phrygian king's touch turned everything into gold?		
9	What was the name of the largest diamond ever found?		
10	What sort of animal is a 'Silverback'?		
		Final Score:	

Allan & Co's

MYSTERY DRIVE
& ROUNDERS MATCH
25th May 2000

BAR MEAL VOUCHER
Hand this voucher in at the Bar
to receive one Bar Meal.

Valid only during the evening of the above event

Allan & Co's

QUIZ RESULTS

25th May 2000

Car or Team Number	Team Members	Final Score	Final Position
1			
2			
3			
4			
5			
6			
7			
8			
9			
10			
11			
12			

The winning team was number: ....

  - Have an empty column on the extreme right in which to enter the marks. A space for the final score should be at the foot of the column.

- **Quiz Answer Sheets,** at least one for each car, assuming that a quiz is taking place. It is better to write the answers in the spaces allocated on a copy of the Quiz Question Sheet and then print off as many copies as may be needed. Whatever happens, don't mix the Answer Sheets with the Question Sheets!

- **Final Score Sheets** to record the results of a quiz or similar pastime. Only one Final Score Sheet may be needed to read out or pin up at the end of the event. If the pastime is one where each car's occupants is a team in its own right, the Score Sheet could be produced in columns and show:

  - the organiser's or organisation's name and the title and date of the event at the top of the sheet.
  - the car (team) number in column 1
  - the names of the team members in column 2
  - the final score attained by each team and
  - the overall position of each team.

- **Meal, Drink, etc. Vouchers** may be necessary, in which case they are best produced on a single-colour card with whatever details you think necessary. To avoid them being mislaid, it is safer to issue them when participants arrive at the starting point. Include:

  - information which restricts their use solely to the one event
  - the organiser's or organisation's name and the date and title of the event
  - the purpose of the voucher (for example, *Get One Drink Free)* and where it must be exchanged.

Leave Nothing to Chance

For your own peace of mind, double-check everything before the event!

- Check the route to make sure nothing has changed, such as an unexpected road diversion. It is useful if someone else navigates using your instructions with another person (not yourself!) driving. You could sit in the back observing and making alterations to the itinerary instructions.
- While they're at it, get them to check the Panic Envelope instructions.
- Check that you have not forgotten anything needed at the venue(s).
- Then amend the instructions if necessary. Produce the requisite number of copies of all the paperwork. It helps if a plastic wallet, one for each car, is prepared and numbered; put everything each car will need inside its particular wallet, e.g. Itinerary sheet(s), Panic Envelope, Car Notice and, if appropriate, the requisite number of meal, drink, etc. vouchers and quiz sheets.
- For double-destination events, prepare a second set of wallets to include Itinerary sheet(s) for the second stage of the drive plus anything else the cars will need.
- Make sure you have everything you need for whatever is scheduled to happen at the venue(s).
- On the morning of the event, make a courtesy call to the venue to ensure they haven't forgotten that your event is taking place and tell them when they may expect the first wave of participants to arrive.
- If you have any doubts about anything to do with the drive or the venue(s), ask questions!

Chapter 7

MYSTERY DRIVES: THE BIG DAY

The Starting Point

Today's the day when all your efforts will be appreciated, assuming you have taken care to make all the necessary preparations and have left nothing to chance.

You should be the first to arrive at the starting point for the drive. Allow yourself a good ten minutes before the first team is due to turn up. Make sure you have everything you need for the duration of the event, including:

- Participants List
- the plastic wallets (one for each stage of the drive for each car) containing Itinerary sheets, Car Notices, Panic Envelopes, vouchers, etc.
- paperwork and anything else required at the destination(s), including money, cheque book, banker's card and items needed for any activity taking place there (if you're responsible for that part of the event. If not, it might be as well to remind the organiser of the destination event to take everything needed, especially prizes.)
- anything else you think you may need, including mobile telephone if you have one.

When each participating car arrives, note the car registration number on your Participants List and hand them their plastic wallet. Tell the occupants to read the notes out loud (so that everyone hears them) before setting off.

Be as helpful as you can if they have any questions but try not to give away any secrets (such as the destination).

Treat all cars equally; don't show any favouritism. Wish them a safe journey and tick them off on the Participants List when they depart.

Repeat the process for each car, allowing about five minutes between each departure.

If any car is late, allow the next one due to leave to take its place and leave a few minutes earlier. When a car arrives late for its scheduled departure time, try to fit it in without inconveniencing those cars which have arrived at their designated time.

When the last car has left, wait for a few minutes before setting off yourself. Follow the same route as those taking part and, if you see one of the driver's cars parked on the side of the road (whether scheduled or not), stop in a safe place nearby and have a brief word.

You could enquire if everything's OK or pass a comment on the view or other features of interest. It doesn't matter, as long as you show a polite interest.

If they have problems, such as uncertainty about your instructions, clarify them to put their minds at ease.

The Venue(s)

It is unlikely that you will be first to arrive at the venue if only because of the length of time it has taken to attend to all the participating cars' departures.

Make your presence known to the owner/manager of the venue and ensure you mention to him any problems which arise straight away to get them resolved as quickly as possible.

By the same token, do your best to keep your group under control in case it affects your chances of making use of the venue again in the future.

Make a point of welcoming everyone when they arrive and help them to settle down. Point out where drinks may be obtained, how to order their meals, etc.

If a fun activity is to take place, tell everyone where they have to go and when the activity will begin (or refer them to the separate organiser of that part of the proceedings).

Make sure things keep moving; do not allow periods of uncertainty or inactivity to arise because it leads to restlessness and boredom.

Before you leave, settle the bill and get a receipt.

The Aftermath

When the event is over, assess how well it has gone by reflecting on observations both you and the participants have made. Invite candid criticism and listen carefully to what is said.

Learn from your experience; do not be afraid to change things in the future if it helps to improve matters and enhance the enjoyment of your participants.

Make a note of aspects which should be included in the next event you organise. Things can only get better...

Finally, send a courtesy letter to the venue itself. If there have been any complaints, pursue them diplomatically. If there haven't, they will appreciate a letter of thanks.

All Clues must be easy to find!

Chapter 8

STANDARD TREASURE HUNTS: CONSIDERATIONS

Most of the considerations concerned with organising a successful Standard Treasure Hunt are similar to those for Mystery Drives as detailed in Chapter Five; use them as a starting point if you haven't already read that chapter.

Because the Treasure Hunt serves a different purpose (it is a competition, not simply a drive along a set route), further aspects must be considered.

- **Who will be taking part?**

The type of people you expect to take part in the hunt may affect the way you devise the clues and influence you in deciding the finishing point.

If your victims are all adults, take into account whether they will tend towards an academic approach to the hunt or, as may be more likely, a more down-to-earth style. Whatever your preconceptions, bear in mind that most ordinary folk often surprise themselves with the amount of general knowledge and common sense they have.

The main aim should be to provide clues of varying complexity so that some are easy, others are quite difficult. After all, the object of the exercise is to result in an overall winning team. However, you don't want to appear too simple minded or arrogant, so try to devise clues which stand a reasonable chance of being solved, in most cases, by the majority of those taking part.

- **Where should the destination be?**

As far as the venue is concerned, it must be capable of accommodating all the people and vehicles taking part together with any special requirements if they are needed. (Does it have facilities for the disabled or children, for example?) Also, will the venue suit most of those taking part? Beware of choosing a place that may be too up- or down-market. Many country pubs are ideal.

The most common requirements for the venue are that it will:

- provide reasonably priced food and drink which will suit everyone (including vegetarians and, perhaps, children)
- be comfortable and in pleasant surroundings with friendly staff
- accommodate the numbers of people and vehicles involved, preferably with a private room where your party can relax undisturbed
- not be too far away from where most of the participants live. (They will not thank you for having to travel a long distance to return home after the event.)

Hunts may not end at a country pubs or similar establishments; you may decide to finish at a country beauty spot or similar. If this is the case, you may want to consider a picnic or barbecue. If you do, the facilities there may be basic or non-existent and the weather inclement.

Choosing such venues can be fraught with problems, especially after the participants have spent a couple of hours on the road. It is much safer to conclude the event at an indoor venue where some comfort can be expected.

- **How long should the hunt take?**

The best hunts usually take no more than two hours from start to finish; any less and the event will hardly be worth doing; any more and the participants will be at each others throats! Much will depend on:

- how long it takes to get from the starting point to the first clue. It may be necessary to drive several miles before the hunt actually begins unless you are able to find a suitable meeting place (for example, somewhere with a car park) not far away from the first clue, in which case you may need to obtain permission from the owner.

- how many clues you decide to have along the route
- how long the actual route is and the nature of the roads and
- how far it is from the final clue to the finishing point.

An overall distance of between 20 and 30 miles with about 30 to 40 clues is reasonable. However, you will need to check the suitability when preparing the hunt (as detailed in the following chapters). An average speed of between ten and fifteen mph is quite normal and, indeed, preferable.

Whatever route you decide must always satisfy the most important consideration: the safety of the participants and other road users.

Do not venture into Churchyards!

Chapter 9

STANDARD TREASURE HUNTS: PLANNING

Planning is the key to a successful Treasure Hunt. Paying attention to the smallest detail must be the main consideration of every organiser. Mistakes and oversights can reduce enjoyment and sometimes cause conflict. Most of the information contained in Chapter Six also applies to planning a Treasure Hunt, so please read it before proceeding with this part of the book.

It is essential to spend as much time as possible devising the hunt and to think constantly about things that could go wrong from the time the event is announced right up to when the participants leave the final venue to return home. They will want to remember the event for the best reasons, not for being a disaster.

Assuming that you have decided where the hunt will commence and where it will end, try to get to know the area between those two points. It will help if relevant large scale (e.g. Landranger series) Ordnance Survey maps are purchased. Examine the maps to see if a suitable route makes itself apparent. Look for potential clue locations; churches, public houses, telephone boxes, etc.

Avoid major roads and motorways unless they are to be used purely as a means of arriving at the first clue or the final venue. Under no circumstances should clues be situated on these types of road because they will present a potential danger to the participants and other road users. Drivers need to be able to concentrate on their driving and the safety of their passengers without having too many distractions.

Also try to avoid twisting or unsurfaced country lanes. Again, these roads require more concentration and it is not a good idea to locate clues along such stretches. Straighter and wider country roads provide fewer hazards, especially if they have lay-bys and passing places.

It can be very useful to drive around the general area to test the roads and availability of suitable clues. It can help to get things clear in your mind. Do not be tempted to decide the route without having first hand knowledge of the roads and conditions. Some roads can seem fine on the map but may be riddled with potential dangers or devoid of sufficient or suitable clues. It's worth spending a little time checking things out before making decisions you may later regret.

Final Venue

Unlike the Mystery Drive, it is not usually a good idea to run another competition (such as a quiz) *after* a Treasure Hunt. As a rule, participants much prefer to relax in comfortable surroundings, have a meal and a drink and talk about their experiences.

It will help if you can canvas opinion from some of the people likely to be taking part to ascertain the sort of venue they would prefer. You could even ask for the names of specific hostelries but do not let anyone know where your chosen venue will be. Not knowing where the hunt will finish is all part of the fun. Just make sure that the venue is suitable and not too far away from the homes of the people who will take part.

As organiser, you will be kept busy marking answer sheets and making sure the catering is as agreed with the proprietor beforehand. It is much better to leave your hunters to amuse themselves without causing more stress to nerves that may already be at breaking point. Being confined in a car with other people while taking part in a hunt can cause tension, so don't be tempted to overload folk with yet another competition afterwards.

The Route

The procedures for planning the route and preparing clue and/or question sheets is much the same as for Mystery Drives with the emphasis placed on finding items on the route for which clues can be devised. Try to avoid routes passing through towns and built up areas where the traffic can be unpredictable and parking difficult. Treasure Hunts in towns require special treatment and are outside the scope of this book.

Creating the clue sheet is the main aim. Not only does it give details of the route itself but also includes clues to be solved at specific points on the way.

Having decided where the route will be, enlist the help of a close friend, spouse or co-organiser and get them to drive the car. Make sure you are armed with all the essential equipment suggested in Chapter Six and warn the driver to proceed slowly and with caution, and be ready to stop at a moment's notice.

Go to the point where the hunt will commence and make a note of the starting mileage. Remember to note the finishing mileage when you arrive at the final venue.

As soon as you set off, make copious notes of the route directions. They must be made very clear. If awkward junctions require some forewarning (e.g. *TAKE THE INSIDE LANE WHEN APPROACHING THE TRAFFIC LIGHTS),* make sure you note them down. It is a good idea to jot directions down in CAPITAL letters so that they are easy to identify when preparing the clue sheets later.

When you are safely away from busy roads, look for your first clue. In practice, most clues relate to man-made features rather than natural objects, although there is no reason why one item should not act as a pointer to another. The problem with nature is that it changes things. Grass and hedges, for example, have a tendency to grow; in doing so they can hide objects which you may want to use as clues or answers. If in doubt, leave it out.

All clues should be visible from within the vehicle. At worst, use one visible object as a signal for participants to get out of their car in order to find the answer to a clue in close proximity but which is itself out of sight. Look behind you and beyond the roadside frequently; some good clues may lurk behind walls and can easily be overlooked but take care when doing so.

The very first clue should be made very simple, as should the first clue after a change of direction; after turning left at a crossroads, for example. Doing so reassures participants and reduces the likelihood of them getting lost. However tempting it may be to try to lose hunters en route, it is neither sportsmanlike nor fair. You will have ample opportunity to cause confusion when devising difficult clues elsewhere on the route.

Other points to bear in mind:

- Only choose clues in safe locations.
- Consider letting the route cross itself, as in an open-ended figure of 8. However, no stretch of road on the hunt itself (i.e. where clues are located) should be repeated.
- All clues must be easy to see (although they may be hard to decipher).
- Observe the Countryside Code and do not trespass.
- Respect the privacy of local residents. Do not have any clues which could cause inconvenience or annoyance to local residents, such as in their gardens, without prior permission from the inhabitant(s).
- Do not venture into churchyards or other places where this type of leisure activity could cause offence.
- Try to devise clues as you go along. If necessary, take photographs of likely candidates (e.g. wordy notices) so that you can give further thought to them later.
- Make sure clues and directional instructions are recorded in the correct order.
- Record more clues than you are likely to need. It is better to have too many than too few. You can delete the ones you don't like or want later.
- Look in village shop windows, look at pub signs, village hall notice boards. In fact, examine everything that won't or is unlikely to move (even drain covers).
- Try to have relatively long stretches between some clues (it can generate panic!) and very short distances between others.

- If you decide you want participants to collect or 'scavenge' objects en route (e.g. a feather, acorn, fir cone, etc.) make sure they exist in adequate quantities and that they will still be available when the hunt is due to take place. Items which are likely to be out of season very quickly (such as wild flowers) should be avoided if you are not sure. Dandelions and daisies are prolific during the summer. Collecting such items must not cause damage to vegetation or property.

- Keep an eye open for notices advertising local events, (such as gymkhanas and point-to-point racing) not so much for using them as clues but in case the event might cause severe congestion on the roads at the time when your hunt is in full swing.

Guidance on suitable items and examples of the types of clues which can be devised for them are detailed later.

When you have concluded the route and made a note of the final mileage, you are ready to return home and prepare the clue sheets and other stationery requirements, using the examples given in Chapter Six (with suitable amendments) as a guide.

Don't forget the cover sheet for the clues, setting out the rules of engagement. The cover sheet should contain:

- Spaces for the car number (and starting and finishing mileage and distance travelled if required, or include them on the first page of the clue sheet).

- Notes on insurance and conduct to cover yourself from liability in case of accident and to reduce the possibility of cheating and unfair play.

- General information on how to find clues and requiring answers to be written in ink, not pencil.

- Notes on how the scoring system works and what happens if the Panic Envelope is opened. For example, 2 points for every correct answer, 1 point for a partially correct answer and no points for an incorrect answer. Opening the Panic Envelope will result in 10 points being deducted from the final score. Also make it clear that the judge's (organiser's) decision is final. Some

ALLAN & Co's
TREASURE HUNT
25th May 2000
COMPETITORS' RULES

Car Number

EVERYONE IN THE CAR SHOULD READ THESE NOTES BEFORE SETTING OFF ON THE QUEST

The Hunt is not a race, but a challenge to see which team is the most observant and best at solving the devious clues.

Your car should be roadworthy and the Highway Code observed at all times. Valid driving licences and insurance cover must exist for everyone who drives during the Hunt.

Particular care should be taken when stopping the car to ensure no obstruction to other road users is caused. Similarly, take care when leaving the car, even on the quieter stretches: always check that there is nothing coming which could cause a danger to yourself, your Team members or other road users.

Also, under no circumstances should you trespass on private property or create a nuisance to residents or animals who live on the route; please respect their privacy. Do not remove or damage any of the clues; to do so is cheating as well as an offence and could lead to disqualification. Everyone involved in the Hunt must have the same chance of winning.

All the route instructions and clues are attached to this sheet. Spaces are provided for your answers, which must be written in ink, not pencil. Read the instructions and clues very carefully.

All the 'treasure' can be seen from the car, although you may need to disembark as some of the answers are quite small; don't forget to lock and alarm your car if everyone gets out for any reason. Remember to look over your shoulder at times: some of the answers may be visible only when you have passed them!

All correct answers are worth 2 points; 1 point may be given for a partially correct answer (at the Judges' discretion). Only one answer may be given for each question; multiple answers will be disregarded, even if one of them happens to be correct. The Judges' decision is final (no arguments, please!). The team with the most points wins. In the event of a tie, the team with the lowest admissible mileage will be declared the winner.

If you are nowhere near finishing the Hunt by ___ o'clock or if there is an emergency and you need to contact the organisers urgently, please open the Panic Envelope. It will tell you where the Hunt ends and give a contact telephone number. Unfortunately, by opening the Panic Envelope you will have 10 points deducted from your final score, but at least you will arrive at the destination.

Please take a few moments to familiarise yourself with the instructions and clues before setting off on your quest. If you need further clarification, ask the organiser now. Once you have set off, you're on your own!

Good luck!

Finishing mileage ________
Starting mileage ________
Distance travelled ________

organisers award variable points depending on the relative complexity of each clue. This can make things awkward when marking and is best avoided.

- A statement on any time limit by which the hunt must be concluded. (This is to ensure everyone arrives at the destination before last meals are served.)

TREASURE HUNT CLUES

DO NOT WRITE IN THE POINTS COLUMN!

During the hunt you should try to find the following items and put them in the plastic bag. Each item handed in is worth 2 points. If you find all five items, 2 bonus points will be awarded.

			Points
1	Origin of large oaks	_______	
2	Luck of the Irish	_______	
3	Container for fiery timber	_______	
4	A heptagon	_______	
5	Permit to travel	_______	
	Bonus points	_______	
	Total		____

TURN LEFT WHEN YOU LEAVE THE STARTING POINT CAR PARK. TURN RIGHT AT THE T JUNCTION. GO STRAIGHT OVER AT THE FIRST SET OF TRAFFIC LIGHTS AND TURN RIGHT AT THE NEXT ROUNDABOUT. CONTINUE ALONG THIS ROAD FOR ABOUT FOUR MILES AND TURN LEFT TOWARDS HUNTLEIGH. GO UNDER THE RAILWAY BRIDGE AND TURN SECOND RIGHT.

1. When is the last time the postman visits on Saturdays? ____________________ ____
2. If Telford = 21, what does Shrewsbury equal? ____________________ ____

TURN LEFT AT T JUNCTION

3. Dial up for Busby's box ____________________ ____

YOU HAVE NOW COMPLETED THE HUNT!

CONTINUE ALONG THIS ROAD UNTIL YOU ARRIVE AT A CROSSROADS. TURN LEFT AND FOLLOW THE ROAD UNTIL YOU SEE THE SECOND PUBLIC HOUSE (MONARCH'S BONCE) ON THE LEFT. ENTER THE CAR PARK. MAKE A NOTE OF YOUR FINAL MILEAGE ON THE FRONT PAGE.

HEAD FOR THE BAR AND HAND YOUR ANSWER SHEETS, PANIC ENVELOPE AND PLASTIC BAG TO THE ORGANISER.

TOTAL SCORE: ________

Once the clue sheets have been drafted, get two friends who will not be taking part in the hunt and whose secrecy can be relied upon to take part in a dummy run. You should sit in the back of the car and observe. You should not offer any advice unless difficulties occur.

The chances are that problems will arise because you have overlooked or taken something for granted. In other words, it's probably your fault.

However, in the light of what transpires, you may need to make amendments to both the directional instructions as well as the clues themselves.

Keep your mind open to suggestions and try not to be too defensive. Remember that the hunt is not for your enjoyment but that of your victims!

Treat the whole thing as a learning experience. Many organisers do not bother to go through this stage and regard it as a waste of time. It shows.

Do not expect your helpers to solve all the clues and be prepared to amend your instructions if something happens which raises doubt about the safety of a clue location. Better to scrap a good clue than cause injury. Similarly, take heed of comments regarding the relevance of a clue to its answer.

After the dummy run has finished, you should know exactly how long the route is and roughly how much time is needed to complete the course.

Try to make the event last for about two hours. If the dummy run takes a lot longer, you will have to consider ways in which to reduce the time, possibly by scrapping some of the clues.

You should then be in a position to prepare the final version of your clue sheets.

Preparing stationery

Follow the advice given in Chapter Six and vary the designs in accordance with your needs and individual circumstances.

Pay particular attention to the clarity of layout and instructions on the clue sheets themselves. It is useful to make all directional instructions in CAPITAL letters centred on the page.

Clues should be numbered consecutively with spaces on the right hand side of the page for entering answers and to note the score for each question, with a space for the overall total at the very end of the last page.

Separate General Knowledge (with a bias towards 'treasure') quiz sheets are worthwhile if there are fairly long

TREASURE HUNT PARTICIPANTS LIST

Date of the Event: ....

First arrival time: ....

Last arrival time: ....

Car Number	Team Members	Entry Fees paid in full (✓)	Car to arrive at (time)	Car Reg. No.	Final Score	Final position in the Hunt
1						
2						
3						
4						
5						
6						
7						
8						
9						
10						
11						
12						

The winning team was in car number ....

stretches of road devoid of clues; they help reduce boredom. A quiz can also put extra pressure on teams because they may cause a distraction, resulting in missed clues.

The Participants List can be used to record the time of arrival at the starting point (as well as details of each car and its occupants), entrance fee payments and final scores, so that all this information is kept on a single form.

The next phase is to advertise the event, sell tickets (one for each person taking part. Consider imposing a maximum number in each team, for example four people including the driver.).

Keep records of fees received and payments made for the purchase of prizes. Make arrangements with the proprietors of the final venue and pay a deposit if required.

Final Checks

Shortly before the day of the hunt, go around the route one last time to make sure that all your instructions and clues are still present and correct.

Remember to take a copy of your clue sheet with you. As with the dummy run, it is preferable for someone else to drive so that you can concentrate on the accuracy of your clue sheets.

Make sure you amend the master copy if necessary and print out as many sets of clue sheets as are needed.

Similarly, print off sufficient sets of the answers so that you can hand them out after everyone has reached the final venue. (One per car plus a few spares is normal.)

Answer sheets can be produced by writing the answers on one of the clue sheets and copying them, or by listing them on a separate piece of paper with the clue number followed by the answer, i.e.

Clue no.	***Answer***
1.	Post box
2.	2.5
3.	Saturdays
etc.	

Don't try to explain each answer on the sheet: it will take too much time!

Finally, have a quiet ponder over your arrangements a few days before the event. Try to think of anything you could have forgotten.

Whatever happens, don't put off your ponderings until the last moment!

Chapter 10

STANDARD TREASURE HUNTS: THE BIG DAY

Before leaving home

Collect everything you will need for the event, including:

- Participants List and score sheet
- clue sheets
- quiz sheets (if appropriate)
- answers for the clue (and quiz) sheets
- a few spare ball point or felt tip pens
- notepad
- plastic bags if participants will be collecting items of 'treasure'
- mobile telephone (if you have one) for emergencies
- map(s) of the hunt area (in case anyone gets lost)
- prizes (bottle of spirits, gift tokens, etc. and perhaps a certificate for the winning team and a booby prize)
- money, cheque book, banker's and/or credit card to pay the bill at the final venue
- camera (if you want to take photos of the event)
- anything else you think you may need
- a full tank of petrol in the car.

Keep all related items together in separate boxes, binders or folders and make sure that all the answer sheets are kept hidden away so that no one sees them.

Give a spare key for your car to a spouse, friend or co-organiser in case yours gets mislaid (ask them to keep it on their person at all times).

Look for Clues behind you – but take care!

The Hunt

Arrive at the starting point before the first team is due to appear and welcome everyone as they turn up.

When each participating car arrives, note the car registration number and the names of all team members on the Participants List.

Hand them their plastic bag (if needed), a clue and, if required, a quiz sheet with their car or team number (from 1 to 12) already written in the spaces provided plus (if this is the way you've organised things) their meal tickets for use at the final venue. Tell them they must all read the instructions carefully before setting off.

Be as helpful as you can without giving any secrets away. Treat all teams equally; don't show any favouritism. Wish them a safe journey and send them on their way.

If any team is late, allow the next team to take their place and leave a few minutes earlier than scheduled. Try to fit in late-comers without inconveniencing those who have arrived at their designated time.

Stagger departure times to avoid bunching en route: about five minute intervals are sufficient.

Wait for a few minutes after the last team has departed, then follow the same route as those taking part. If you overtake any team before they reach the first clue, wait nearby until you are sure that they are on the right track.

If you have chosen a figure of 8 route, observe things from the intersection. Otherwise, follow the full course and stop whenever you come across a team.

Ask if everything is OK and show some interest in their progress without offering advice unless they are absolutely desperate. In any event, do not give them too much help; it is unfair on the other teams. Use your discretion.

The Final Venue

It is probable that you will arrive at journey's end before any of the participants.

Make yourself known to the proprietor and check that everything is ready for when your guests to arrive. Go to the venue room and find a table near to the entrance so that you can greet everyone when they turn up.

Have your answer sheet ready to check the completed clue sheets and get yourself a drink. Take advantage of a few moments of peace and quiet before the onslaught begins.

As each team arrives, welcome them and take their clue (and possibly quiz) sheets, panic envelope and plastic bag of treasure. Tell them to get a drink and order their meal. Mark each team's answers in the order in which they are handed in and hold on to them until the last one has been marked. Be consistent in the way you allocate marks for partially correct answers.

Politely refrain from telling teams what their score is until the whole job has been completed; it adds to the suspense. Enter the final scores on the Participants List and work out the order of their respective positions.

As soon as you are ready (they will all want to know the outcome), get everyone's attention, thank them for coming and say that you hope they all had an enjoyable time. Also say that you hope someone else will organise the next hunt (a hint that you'd like to take part instead of organising).

Announce the results in reverse order and hand out the prizes. Return the clue sheets with an answer sheet to each team and pin up the Participants List showing the scores for everyone to see.

Then relax, if you can. There are bound to be a few objections to your scoring criteria, but you are the judge and your rulings (provided they are consistently fair) should be accepted.

Similarly, you may be asked about specific clues and answers. Be prepared for all sorts of questions and give honest answers. The organiser is, after all, the only one who knows the reasons why and how clues were devised.

Finally, settle the invoice with the proprietor, get a receipt and thank him or her and the staff for all their help. Remember to dispose of all your rubbish (including the plastic bags containing 'treasure') sensibly.

The Aftermath

When the event is over but still fresh in your mind, reflect on how well or how badly things have gone. Take into account your own observations together with the comments made by your victims. Invite candid criticism and do not take offence at any honest appraisal.

Make notes and keep all your paperwork in a safe place so that they can be referred to when the next hunt is organised or if anyone else seeks advice on the subject. Learn from your mistakes. The next event will be that much better...

Finally, send a courtesy letter to the final venue. If there have been any complaints about the service or facilities, pursue them diplomatically. If all went well, they will appreciate a letter of thanks.

Respect the Privacy of Local Residents!

Chapter 11

SCATTER EVENTS

The organisation of a Scatter Event is almost identical to that for a Standard Treasure Hunt but generally requires less time to prepare the clue sheets. This is because a Scatter Event does not have a fixed route.

As far as planning is concerned, organisers should familiarise themselves with the chapters relating to both Mystery and Standard Treasure Hunts and proceed to plan along the guidelines given.

The organiser, having ascertained the starting point and final venue, must decide on (say) twelve locations from which participating teams will choose no more than nine (how many up to nine is up to you) to visit.

They will be required to find the answer to a single clue relating to and which will necessitate a visit to each of their chosen locations.

Their vehicles are used to reach each location and participants should need to disembark and search around in order to find and solve the clues.

Sounds simple? Well, not really.

The clue sheet for Scatter Events is best divided into columns. The first column contains a cryptic clue to each of the twelve locations. In the second column, alongside each cryptic clue, is another clue pertaining to that location. A third column is for the scores.

Participants will first need to try and ascertain the names of as many of the locations as possible (for which they will be awarded points for correct answers, even though they are not required to visit them all) and then decide which of them they will visit.

The other decision they will have to make is the order in which their chosen places will be visited so that each specific locational clue may be solved. The answers to these

ALLAN & Co's

SCATTER TREASURE HUNT: CLUE SHEET
25th May 2000

PLACE NAME	CLUE FOR THAT LOCATION	POINTS (for organiser's use only)
GR SJ = Multiply William's year of conquest by a baker's dozen, then add the year England's footballers won the World Cup and multiply by the number of days in March. Answer:	Red light food Answer:	
Mailman's workplace not at low pig joint. Answer:	Last collection on Saturdays? Answer:	
ROPER ISLE Answer:	What was built in MCMLXVII? Answer:	
The first part of this place is really not old; the second is where ships may be sold. Answer:	Who is allowed to use this car park? Answer:	
GEEARRREYEENNDEEELLEEEWHY Answer:	Where to find us? Answer:	
Duke's Domain Answer:	What can you have with morning coffee at the station? Answer:	
10100 - 00101 - 01100 - 00110 - 01111 - 10010 - 00100 Answer:	Graffiti on the buses? Answer:	
Dragon slayer's? Answer:	Name the fourth house Answer:	
Lanthanum + Potassium + Einsteinium = Answer:	Nutcrackers? Answer:	
XIX - VIII - IX - XVI - XX - XV - XIV Answer:	Invoice for shelter Answer:	
If Dawley = 6, Ketley = 2 and Dothill = 1, where is it? Answer:	What gem has the solution? Answer:	
Aleman's acorn source Answer:	How many pales around Lister's dogs home? Answer:	
FINAL DESTINATION	Monarch's bonce at the Shakespeare tragedy Answer:	
	FINAL SCORE	

locational clues should attract higher scores than solving those in the first column.

From the practical point of view, it is sometimes necessary for teams to visit more than nine locations if they are unable to solve the clue given for a particular place. The object of the exercise is for them to find the answers to nine and only nine locational clues: they will not gain extra points for solving more than nine but, of course, will lose points if they solve less than nine. However, they will be able to gain a few extra points if they can successfully solve more than nine of the cryptic clues in column one of the clue sheet.

Because there is no set route for this type of event, it follows that there is no minimum or maximum expected mileage. Similarly, there should be no need to encourage speeding by imposing time restrictions other than the customary *if you are nowhere near finishing before a given time, proceed to the final venue.*

Sometimes it is worth adding an extra cryptic clue to say where the final venue is located. If this is the case, then a Panic Envelope should be provided stating and including a simple map of the location. In these circumstances, points will be deducted from the team's score if the envelope is opened or tampered with.

Planning Scatter Events

As with other events, decide where the starting point and final venue will be and make whatever arrangements are necessary concerning permissions and catering.

Then plan the hunt. This is best done by purchasing an Ordnance Survey (or similar) map of the area. Unlike Standard Treasure Hunts, there is no need to go to the trouble of planning a route.

Instead, choose twelve locations, preferably villages or places of particular interest, all of which are on the same map sheet if possible.

No location should be more than about five miles from another and, if it is feasible, all twelve locations will fall within a radius of about twenty miles from either the starting point or final venue (which could, of course, be the same place).

The organiser should then visit every location and decide on a clue specific for each. It helps if each clue is appropriate to an easily recognisable feature at the location, such as a public house, post office, village hall, notice boards outside dominant buildings, telephone or letter boxes, etc., but it is not essential for every clue. It is also useful to devise a second clue as a backup in case the original seems inappropriate at a later time.

Do not make two similar clues for two different locations; try to vary the type of each clue to add mental interest to the problem solving.

If one of the locations appears to be unsuitable for one reason or another, choose a replacement. When all the locations seem satisfactory, prepare the clue sheet in accordance with the advice given at the beginning of this chapter.

Cryptic Place Name Clues

These clues should vary in difficulty so that there is an equal mix of hard and simple clues. All clues, however, should be solvable by anyone prepared to give a little thought to the processes required to work out the answers.

The easiest clues to solve are those in the form of grid references, anagrams and phonetics.

- **Grid References**

If you state the Ordnance Survey grid reference (for example, GR SK123456) of a location, every team should be able to determine it by referring to the example included on the Ordnance Survey map itself.

Indeed, the clue to be solved at that location could very well be at that exact grid reference. Otherwise it might simply relate generally to the centre of the village.

Note that grid reference numbers are always preceded by the letters GR and the two letters allocated (by the Ordnance Survey) to the map sheet in CAPITALS (SK in the example above).

Another way of rendering a grid reference is to set a simple mathematical sum (which can itself be encrypted) to provide the GR number.

For example, *GR SK = Multiply William's conquering year by a baker's dozen, add the year England's footballers won the World Cup and multiply by the number of days in March,* i.e. 1066 x 13 + 1966 x 31 = GR SK490544.

- **Anagrams**

People who like crosswords usually enjoy solving anagrams. Try to devise an anagram using the letters which constitute the place name. For example, an anagram of 'Priorslee' could be *ROPER ISLE.*

If you have use of a computer, there are several cheap anagram-solving and -devising programs available; otherwise it's down to trial and error using pen and paper. Always double check to ensure you don't repeat a letter by mistake.

By convention, show anagrams in CAPITAL letters.

- **Phonetics**

This process involves using three letters to spell out each letter of the place name. These clues are always written in CAPITAL letters (which can cause fun if participants think they are anagrams). For example, the village of 'Grindley' could be clued as *GEEARREYEENNDEEELLEEEWHY.*

Other clues, which may take a little longer to decipher, are as follows. Where it would help if teams had access to the different types of alphabet conversions, there is no reason why the organiser should not give them copies of the charts.

- **Binary Digit Alphabet**

On the face of it, these look impossible to solve but can be deciphered relatively easily when the principles involved are recognised.

Each letter of the cryptic clue is translated as a binary digit alphabet number made up of zeros and ones, with hyphens or spaces and normal punctuation marks separating them where appropriate.

For example, the clue for 'Telford' would be *10100 - 00101 - 01100 - 00110 - 01111 - 10010 - 00100.*

The binary digit alphabet is shown in the appendices and is a relatively simple code to decipher.

- **Sliding Alphabet**

Clues using this simple code are devised as follows. Write the full alphabet (A to Z) down in a single long line. Then write out the alphabet again beneath (or alongside) it, starting with the letter A below any letter other than the

A in the top (or side) row. Continue in order until a letter appears under the letter Z, then continue the run from the top A until the full alphabet has been used.

Then write the clue down in CAPITAL letters and, using the conversion chart, treat the clue letters as belonging to those in the first row and substitute them for the coded letter listed beneath (or alongside) each one.

For example, if the A in the first row corresponds with the letter N in the second row and B equals O, then Z will equal M.

The cryptic clue may thus read: *If A = N, B = O and Z = M, what is FARQ'F UVLL?* (Answer: Sned's Hill.)

A sample Sliding Alphabet with spaces to produce your own is included in the appendices.

- **Roman Numeral Alphabet**

Use the same idea as the binary digit alphabet except that A is depicted as the Roman numeral I (one), B as II (two), right through to Z as XXVI (twenty-six). Any numbers appearing in the clue should, of course, be spelled out as words before translation.

Each word should be separated by hyphens or spaces and normal punctuation marks where appropriate. For example, *VIII - IX - XII - XII XX - XV - XVI* will translate as 'Hill Top'.

Roman numerals are shown in the appendices.

- **Morse Code Alphabet**

Unless at least one person in each team is familiar with Morse Code or has easy access to a Morse Code conversion chart (one is included in the appendices), this is not really worthwhile considering.

Morse Code is now no longer used as a system of communication, although it will probably be included in reference books for a long time to come.

- **Specialist Alphabets**

These may comprise symbol groups, such as Semaphore or Runic characters, used to substitute for the normal English alphabet.

They should only be included if competitors are familiar with them. If not, conversion charts must be provided.

- **Element Tables**

At the time of writing, there are 105 known elements, each with its own alphabetic symbol and atomic weight number. These alphabetic symbols can be used to make up words in their own right and may be referred to by either their elemental name or atomic weight.

For example, the word 'Lakes' can be encrypted as either *Lanthanum + Potassium + Einsteinium =* or *Atomically speaking, 57 + 19 + 99 =.*

Conversion charts for elements, their symbols and atomic weights are shown in the appendices, but it is not a good idea to use them in clues unless you are sure that each team has access to them.

- **Signposts**

These entail a little artistic ability but are quite easy to produce. Imagine a signpost with two or three pointers with the traditional circular (sometimes mint-with-the-hole) shape at the top. The circular shape usually has the name of the place where the signpost has been erected.

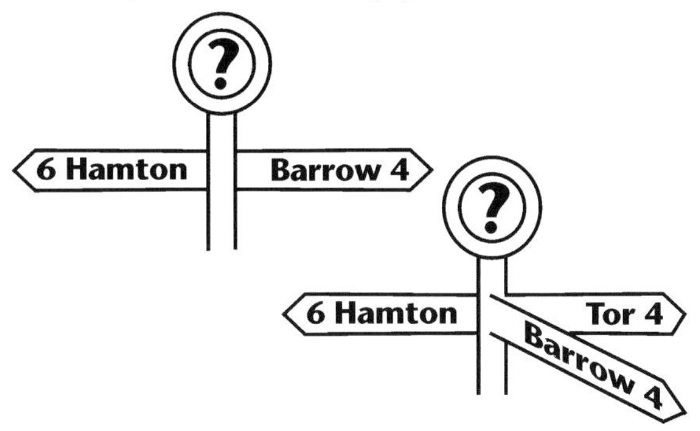

Referring to your map, decide on one of your chosen places. Note how far it is from two or three nearby places in different directions and write them into the relevant pointers of your signpost drawing.

Draw a question mark in the circle; participants should be able to find the name by measuring the distances (as the crow flies) between the place names given on the pointers until they find the chosen place.

When measuring the distances on the map, make sure you use the right scale.

- **Straightforward Clues**

These may be used in between more difficult cryptic clues but try not to use more than six out of the total of twelve. This means that every team must decipher at least three of the more difficult clues in order to reach their total of nine locations.

Straightforward clues are ones which rely on words to describe or point to a given place. If you are that way inclined, you might try to devise a two or four line rhyme to describe the location. For example, 'Newport' might be described as *The first part of this place is really not old; the second is where ships may be sold.* Alternatively, simple word associations may provide the clue: a place called 'Brewer's Oak' could be *Alemaker's acorn source.*

Locational Clues

Having completed the task of producing cryptic place name clues, the next stage is to devise a clue for something to be discovered at each location. These are known as locational clues and appear on the clue sheet in column two alongside the relevant place name in column one.

The organiser should put him or herself in the position of the victims. They have successfully solved the cryptic place name clues but may have no idea exactly where they have to go in their (up to) nine chosen locations.

One way around this is to include the precise position when devising the cryptic clue, for example *Priorslee Post Office* specifies the Post Office at Priorslee. Another way is to include a reference to the precise position in the locational clue itself, such as *Mailman's workplace* (which hints at a Post Office as opposed to a Post Box).

Having pointed out the exact spot in the place, devise an appropriate clue. The type of information to be found can be precisely the same as for any clue given in a Standard Treasure Hunt. The point is that each team must visit the places to find the answers: they should not be able to solve locational clues without actually going there or getting out of their vehicle.

ALLAN & Co's
SCATTER TREASURE HUNT RULES
25th May 2000

Car Number

EVERYONE IN THE CAR SHOULD READ THESE NOTES BEFORE SETTING OFF ON THE QUEST

The Hunt is not a race but a challenge to see which team is the most observant and best at solving the devious clues.

Your car should be roadworthy and the Highway Code must be observed at all times. Valid driving licences and insurance cover must exist for everyone who drives during the Hunt. The safety of all team members rests with the driver/owner of each car; the organiser cannot be held responsible for loss or damage to persons or property sustained whilst the Hunt is in progress.

Particular care should be taken when stopping the car to ensure no obstruction is caused to other road users. Similarly, take care when leaving the car, even on the quieter stretches. Always check that there is nothing coming which could harm yourself or other road users. It is strongly recommended that the driver concentrates on the driving and other team members try to solve the clues.

Also, under no circumstances should you trespass on private property or create a nuisance to residents who live on or near your route; please observe their right to privacy. Nor should you damage, move or hide any of the clues; it's not fair on other competitors and offenders will find their team disqualified from the event.

All the clues are attached to this sheet. Spaces are provided for your answers, which must be written in ink, not pencil. Every clue can be seen from the car although you may need to disembark as some of the answers may be quite small.

There are 12 cryptic clues to the names of places. Each place has a question which can only be solved by visiting that location. You will be awarded 5 points for every place correctly identified and 10 points for every correct question answered. Partially correct answers will be awarded reduced points at the judge's discretion (no arguments, please!). **Note: You need only supply the answers to 8 of the questions, so you do not have to visit all 12 locations.** It is up to you to decide which places to visit and the order in which they are visited. If you are unable to find the answer in one of the places, you may want to visit another to compensate and make up points. You must also solve the cryptic clue to the Final Destination so that you know where to go when you have finished the hunt.

Only one answer is permitted for each location or clue; multiple answers will be disregarded, even if one of them happens to be correct. The team with the most points wins.

If you are nowhere near finishing by _____ o'clock or if there is an emergency and you need to seek help urgently, or if you cannot solve the clue to the final destination, open the Panic Envelope. The contents will tell you where the Hunt ends and give you an emergency telephone number. Unfortunately, by opening the Panic Envelope you will have 10 points deducted from your team's final score but at least you will arrive at the destination.

Please take a few moments to familiarise yourself with the instructions and solve at least one of the cryptic place clues before setting off on your quest. If you need further clarification, ask the organiser now. Once you set off, you're on your own!

Good luck – and have a safe journey.

Other preparations

After completing the clue sheets, produce a covering sheet setting out the rules of the hunt. Also produce all the stationery required as detailed in Chapter Six, with appropriate amendments owing to the nature of this type of event.

There is normally no need to have a dummy run for scatter events but, just to satisfy your doubts, there is no reason why a trustworthy friend or relative should not have a go. Remember to listen to any comments they might make.

The event should proceed generally in accordance with the advice given in Chapter Ten. One major difference is that every team should be provided with the same Ordnance Survey (or similar) map.

Bearing in mind that copyright is reserved, it is not a good idea to produce photocopies (partly because vital information, such as the grid reference points and key to symbols, could be omitted). The cost of these maps could form part of each participant's or team's entry fee.

A good scatter event will, like the Standard Treasure Hunt, last for about two hours. The main difference between these two types of hunt is that teams will spend a fair bit of time deciphering the cryptic place name clues before setting off in their vehicles.

For this reason alone it is a good idea to make a club or public house the starting point. The teams can all assemble at the same time and occupy separate tables while they solve the clues to see where they must go. During this time they may take light refreshment and ask advice from the organiser who should keep them under control to minimise time wasting.

When each team is ready to leave, they may do so in their own time; there is no need to specify departure times. Some teams will be able to find the place names faster than others so there is no point in making them leave in a particular order.

When all the teams have set off, the organiser does not need to follow them; they will probably scatter (hence the name) in all directions.

What the organiser must do is make sure he or she arrives at the final venue before the competitors.

Chapter 12

VARIATIONS

Having seen how normal types of hunts may be organised, there is always room for embellishment. Some variations work better than others; some may never be successful. This chapter details a few of the enhancements commonly used. Beginners, however, should try their hand at the basic forms of hunt before getting too adventurous.

Some variations are suitable for inclusion in both Standard as well as Scatter Hunts; others are only suitable for the Standard Hunt, mainly because there is a predetermined route to be followed. As a rule, these additions (except for quizzes) are not practical for Mystery Drives.

Alternatives for both types of hunt

Short Quizzes

A quiz in addition to the main clue sheet can help pass the time on longer stretches of road where there are no clues, such as on the drive to the first clue and from the last clue to the final venue.

Quizzes with questions based on 'treasure' in its widest sense are appropriate (there are examples in the appendices), but there is no reason why they should not be of a more general nature. The subject matter is up to you and your perceptions of your victims' abilities.

Questions of varying complexity are the norm with no more than about twenty on a single side of paper. Allow space for the answers and scores and produce an overall score and relative positions sheet to summarise the results.

Although the points attained could be added to the overall score of the hunt itself, it is probably preferable to treat the quiz as another event and award separate prizes to the winning team and runners up.

Remember to provide answer sheets and allow more time at the final venue for marking the papers. It helps if someone else is given the quiz marking to do while the organiser marks the clue sheets for the hunt itself.

Reverse Parking Test

Additional time should be allocated at the starting point if this variation is adopted. Space must also be included on the clue sheet to enter the points scored.

The object of the exercise is to get each participating car to reverse into a parking space on the car park. The parking space should have several traffic cones (obtained legally!) positioned along the sides and far end of the space.

With all members of the team present in the car, the driver must reverse into the space without touching any of the cones. 10 points can be awarded if successful.

If the car touches any cone, 2 points are lost and the driver must try again, and so on until the reverse parking is successful or there are no points left (i.e. after five failed attempts).

Pick a Bottle

Organisers sometimes include a bottle or can of beer or other refreshment as one of the items of treasure to be acquired, assuming there is an off licence, public house or supermarket en route.

These bottles (provided they are full and unopened!) can be used as prizes at the end of the event. However, they constitute additional expenditure to the participants which may not be warmly welcomed.

If it is intended to include items to be paid for as part of the hunt, make sure you warn everyone well before the event and give them a rough idea how much cost is involved.

Paying a Visit

Requiring competitors to pay an entrance fee to a site or attraction (such as national Heritage and Trust properties) in order to solve clues should be avoided. Not only does this constitute additional expenditure but will undoubtedly cause delay and add to the time taken to complete the course. Furthermore, the owners or custodians of these places may not approve of them being used for treasure hunt purposes.

If you desperately want to make use of an entrance fee site, consider using one as a final venue (if it has all the facilities required) but make sure the custodians fully approve. Include the entrance fee as part of the entry fee for the hunt.

Alternatives for Standard Hunts only

Retrospective Clues

When compiling clues, it can be fun to include a question relating to an item or place passed by the teams some distance before the clue appears on the clue sheet. It makes an additional test of their observational powers.

The best examples are things with some form of visual impact, such as an inn sign. Rather than devise a clue for the location at the time when each team approaches the pub, ask a question about it several miles or clues further down the route, like:

How many horse shoes were visible on the pub sign you passed two miles back? or *Name every public house you have passed since the first clue.*

Short Walks

It is not always a good idea to include clues which require competitors to take short walks away from their vehicles. Unattended vehicles at remote locations are susceptible to loss or damage, apart from which no one will thank you for making them venture out if the weather is inclement (and it will be!).

Clues should be readily identifiable from within each vehicle and require a walk of only a few yards at most to ascertain answers. It is better (and quicker) if the majority of answers can be deduced without having to leave the car.

Excessive Mileage Deductions

Sometimes organisers impose penalties for every tenth of a mile travelled in excess of the optimum distance for the hunt. This is not a good idea, for several reasons.

Not every car is fitted with a milometer or trip clock registering tenths of a mile. Furthermore, the imposition of such penalties encourages drivers to travel illegally in reverse (thus reducing their recorded mileage) along stretches of road. Doing so is both stupid and unsafe.

If mileage is to be recorded, it is much better to refer to overall mileage only when there is a tie in the scores for first or other position. Even then, there may be some drivers who think it's clever to cut down on recorded mileage by reversing their vehicle unnecessarily. The fact is that it's illegal, so don't encourage it.

Photographic Clues

It can add more interest to a hunt if photographic clues are included. To do so, it is usual to put all photographs on a

Details for photo clues

Answer:
White House Hotel

Original photo

Answer:
Save petrol station

Original photo

separate question sheet and insert a line under each picture for competitors to enter the name of the building, place or feature from which each photograph was taken.

An even better idea is to select relatively small items to photograph, such as a light fitting, an unusual artefact or a close up detail from a feature which will be difficult to identify when not seen in context with the building (or whatever) to which it is attached.

Because articles are more difficult to identify in black and white than when seen in their normal colours, consider photocopying the photographs when they have been pasted onto a sheet of paper, or convert them from colour into black and white or greyscale using a scanner attached to a computer with suitable software.

A scanner will enable you to crop the pictures to only those parts needed. Other computer software can be used to lay out the page electronically so that it looks better than the cut – paste – photocopy procedure.

Do not lay the photographs out in the order in which they will appear en route; jumble them up. Make each photograph about 8 centimetres square and have four or five on one side of a sheet of paper. Award a few more points than for normal clues and make space for the points awarded in the overall score part of the clue sheet.

Registration Spotting

It might seem a good idea to award points to teams for recording the registration numbers of other vehicles taking part in the hunt.

Such a practice is not to be encouraged; those setting off first will be disadvantaged or tempted to linger along the route, thus causing potential congestion and a danger to other road users.

It's not worth the effort, so don't be tempted.

Exact Mileage Pointers

Some organisers enter the exact mileage of each clue from the starting point as a guide to competitors.

While this information is extremely useful, there seems little point in doing so unless everyone taking part is an absolute novice. It takes away much of the uncertainty and makes things too easy.

Giving the approximate mileage for changes of direction is a slightly different matter and can be a useful tool, especially if the route is not straightforward.

As a general rule, however, quoting mileage information tends to reduce the challenge and enjoyment of the event.

Chapter 13

CANDIDATES FOR CLUES

Some general advice on devising clues has already been given. This chapter examines just a few of the types of items to look out for and how clues for them can be devised.

Because there are so many objects prevalent in the countryside, the most this book can do is point out the more common features. Organisers and participants should bear in mind that the possibilities are endless, as are the innumerable ways in which clues may be phrased.

When constructing a clue, remember the advice given earlier, especially when it is beneficial to make the first clue after a change of direction more obvious and simple to solve than the remainder.

Devising devilish clues is one of the most enjoyable aspects of producing a hunt, from the organiser's point of view.

However, the perceived capability of the participants as a whole should be taken into account but never underestimated. That is why there should be a mixture of simple, harder and decidedly difficult clues to satisfy all tastes.

It helps to produce an overall winner, if nothing else. People like a challenge yet at the same time like to think they stand a chance of winning. And so they should.

'Treasure' Items

If you require teams to collect specific items en route, make sure (as far as you can) that all objects are available in sufficient quantities to satisfy all teams.

There is little point in asking them to bring back some sheep's wool when you have only seen one clump hanging from barbed wire on the whole of the route. (Actually, in this instance you would have to accept any item of woollen clothing as well as natural yarn, but the point is there.)

Furthermore, take into account that seasonal changes can mean that a natural object you see while planning the hunt may not be around when the event itself takes place.

In addition to things appearing naturally in the countryside, consider objects which may be acquired by looking in bus shelters, railway stations, public house and other readily accessible buildings. Make sure that they will be open on the day and time the hunt takes place.

Some examples of treasure, together with suggested clues, are listed in the appendices.

Telephone boxes

Telephone boxes are widespread and it can be surprising to see how many different clues may be devised from such a small object. Take a look inside when you next see one.

As well as the telephone itself, you should see instructions on how to make a call and a chart of dialling codes (depending on whether or not the box has been vandalised).

You could ask competitors to call a specific number for the answer to a clue, in which case make sure you have arranged for the person on the receiving end to give a password as the answer. A possible clue might be *Ten pence and (the telephone number); what's the password.* Participants should recognise that a public telephone is needed, so they will look out for one.

You could ask for *Beaty's code* for a particular town. Or simply put *01952 = where?.* Just make sure the required code is on the chart. Don't use telephone directories or yellow pages in case they are stolen or damaged before or during the event.

The instruction chart also has endless possibilities. The location and number of the telephone should appear, as well as how to make SOS Emergency calls and Operator Service details. Also see if there is any amusing (and repeatable!) graffiti which can be used. Use your ingenuity.

Competitors should always stop to look at telephone boxes. They are prime candidates for clue locations. It is up to you to decide just how difficult your clue will be.

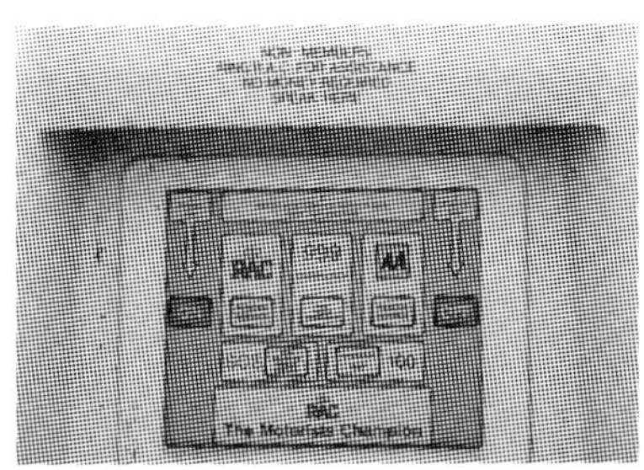
RAC
AA

RAC

343
AA

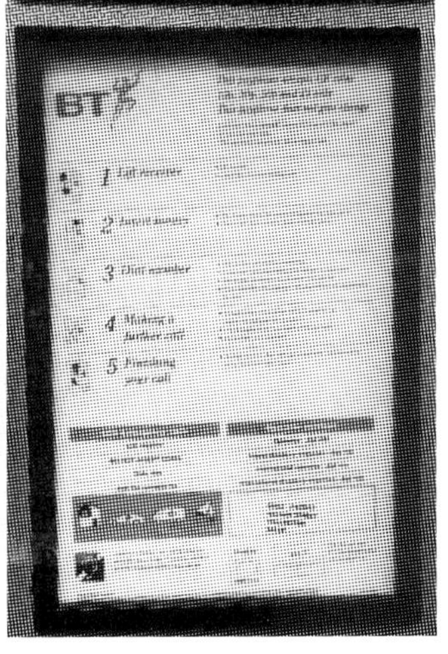
BT

The RAC and AA motoring associations also have their own emergency telephone boxes for the exclusive use of members. They have similar possibilities, but only devise clues to what is visible from the outside. Do not ask competitors to make actual calls from RAC or AA telephones.

Post Boxes

These may be the standard red Pillar Boxes or, more frequently in the countryside, small red rectangular boxes struck on poles. They may even be embedded within walls.

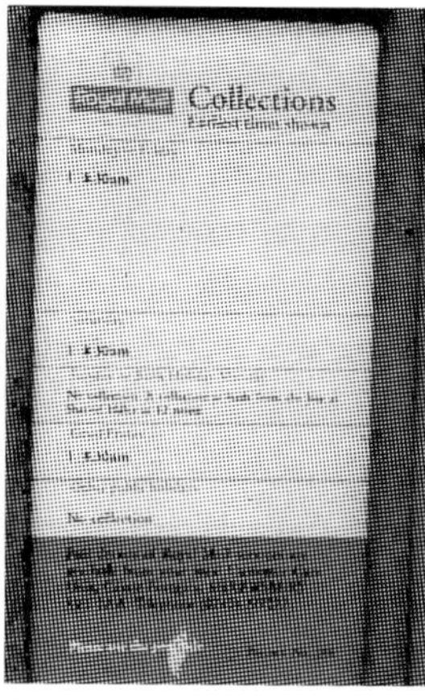

In addition to the square plate showing the next collection number (or day) and the crown and motif of the ruling monarch when the box was manufactured, post boxes usually have a notice giving the days and earliest times of collection, how full details of Royal Mail services can be obtained for that area and a unique 'Postbox No'.

Clues may range from the simple *When is the collection taken on Good Friday* to *What's the telephone number for box no. 123?*. If the phrase 'LETTERS ONLY' appears, consider *QWERTY~~123456~~* as a clue.

Also consider asking for the name of the company who made the post box; on pillar boxes it is usually embossed at the rear of the black-painted base. Most are inscribed with the manufacturer's name *Cannon Company, Stirlingshire.*

Public Houses and Hotels

You would be quite unlucky not to find at least one public house or hotel on your route. It's almost worth varying the route just to include one, especially if it has a feature which offers a great clue.

Things to look out for in particular are:

- pictorial inn signs, especially where there is fine detail, such as in coats of arms which may also have mottoes
- licensee boards (above the main entrance)
- the name of the brewery to which the inn belongs

- notice boards showing facilities, attractions, (credit card) payment information and parking restrictions
- any other interesting items, such as decorative garden, play area and rustic features. Keep an eye open for small details.

Apart from simply asking for the name of the establishment, try to think up clues connected with the inn sign (assuming there is one hanging outside). A common question to ask is *How many legs are hanging around the hostel-*

ry? if the sign includes pictures of people and/or animals. Don't forget to include legs on the other side of the sign if it's free hanging! And check to see if there are any duplicates of the main sign.

Public houses and hotels can be useful places in which to obtain treasure, like bottles of beer, beer mats (always ask for permission from the landlord), small bags of sugar (often served with tea and coffee), etc.

Although hotels have been included in these examples, bear in mind that some have attitudes towards treasure hunters whose attentions may not always be welcome. There's no harm in asking, especially if it means additional trade will come their way.

Notice Boards

There are all sorts of notice boards which lend themselves to clue making. They appear almost anywhere: outside churches, village halls, farms, business premises, petrol stations, railway stations, bus shelters, information points, private property, club houses, public houses, hotels, cottage hospitals, Heritage and Trust sites, recreational facilities, lay-bys, parking areas...

Notice boards offer a wealth of opportunity for clue derivation. Even the colour of the paint work can come in useful, especially if you need to draw attention to a specific notice board when there are several in close proximity.

Be on the look out for notices incorporating pictograms and logos in addition to text. Small detail is often overlooked when competitors are searching for that elusive answer.

Depending on your ingenuity in devising clues, suitable subject matter on notice boards may include:

- name of the establishment
- location, ownership and contact names, addresses, telephone numbers and affiliations
- times and dates of opening, service or events
- services and facilities provided
- prohibitions, restrictions and instructions

Welcome to
Boscobel House
English Heritage
Opening Hours
Open today until 6pm
English Heritage members free

THE NATIONAL TRUST
LITTLE MORETON HALL
HOUSE & GARDEN OPEN
OCTOBER
PLEASE NO INDOOR PHOTOGRAPHY
NO SHARP HEELED SHOES

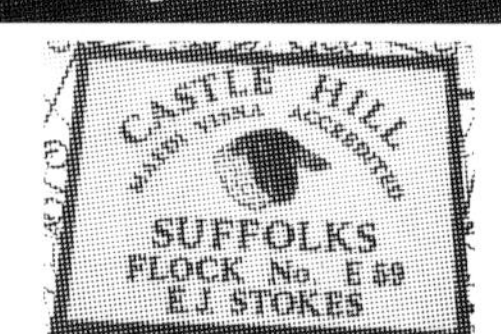
CASTLE HILL
SUFFOLKS
FLOCK No. E 59
E.J. STOKES

KEEP OUT
THIS AREA IS COVERED BY
SECURITY
CAMERAS

And Opposite
Bus Stop
NORTH

WHEATON ASTON HALL
Care for the Elderly
Tel. (0785) 840423

PRIVATE
NO FISHING
NO PICNICS
PATRONS
ONLY

FAMILY
SERVICE
this
SUNDAY
11:00am
SUNDAY WORSHIP
1st Sunday
11:00am Family Service
2nd Sunday
6-30pm Evening Service
3rd Sunday
9-30am Holy Communion
4th & 5th Sundays
9-30am Morning Service

- payment, entrance and special offer details
- historical and social information
- mottoes, pictograms, photographs, maps and plans
- and other types of information not mentioned here...

Don't use *For Sale* or *To Let* notices in case they are removed before or during the hunt. In fact, don't use any signs likely to disappear at a moment's notice, especially the one advertising the Gymkhana which took place last month!

There are many other types of notice which, although not strictly notice boards, can be used in exactly the same way.

They are to be found everywhere and can range in size from very small to quite large. Some in close proximity may be related, as with the notices affixed to the outside of electricity sub-stations.

Look for notices in places such as village post offices, petrol stations, garages and stores as well as those listed above. The sides of agricultural buildings are also good places to look. Manufacturer notices are quite common on the sides of barns, for example.

Road Signs

As a general rule, road signs should not be used as clues; their purpose is to warn and instruct drivers without complicating things unnecessarily.

There are some exceptions (see Directional Clues below), such as signs like 'No Entry Except for Access' which could be clued as *Whose credit is excluded?* (Answer: ACCESS)

Poles and Posts

The countryside features many different sorts of poles and posts, mainly erected by the public utility companies.

Wooden telegraph (telephone) posts often have small oval metal plaques nailed to them. The plaque may have the word 'COBRA' with a number (like 1556) embossed. *(Which serpent supports Beaty?)* These poles may have letter and/or number plaques nailed into them as well, such as W3, FWV and LA13. Successive poles may be numbered W4, W5, etc.. Occasionally a number may be omitted from the sequence. If, as in this example, W6 is missing, a clue might be *W3, W4, W5, ___ . What number is posted next?*

Lamp posts may also have consecutive letters and numbers, such as Z427, Z428, etc. They are also suitable for sequential number clues.

Beware of overhead power lines: each pole supporting them should have a yellow 'Danger of Death' plate with a man lying beneath a lightning bolt within a black triangle. Below the yellow plaque should be a white notice giving an emergency telephone number. If you are tempted to use this as a clue *(What number should you call if you have a shocking experience?)*, the notice should be easily readable without competitors having to climb the pole.

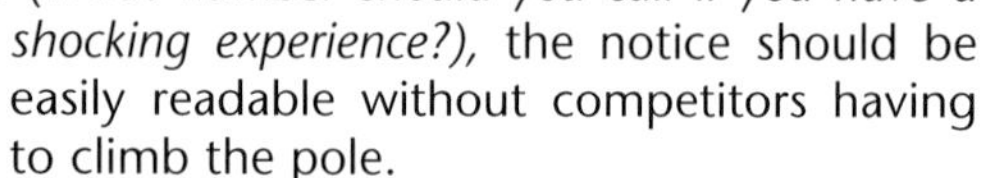

Bus stop signs are usually fixed to poles and posts and sometimes include a bus motif and the name of the bus operator and their telephone number for bus information. If there are several on the route of the hunt, the chances are that they will all be identical.

Water, gas and electricity companies make frequent use of small concrete marker posts set in the ground. Each one has a coloured metal plaque (white, red and blue, although other colours may be used) fixed to the front.

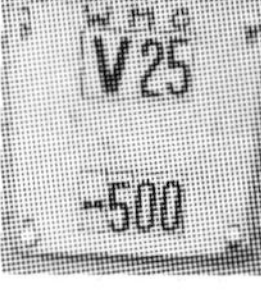

The plaques usually include a combination of numbers and letters and sometimes the initials of the company to whom they belong, such as 'WMG' for West Midlands Gas. The numbers relate to distances from the post; although mainly in metric (1.5 metres) there are still some with Imperial measurements in existence (11′ 6″).

Fire hydrant markers (yellow square plaques featuring a large black letter H and metric numbers) can also be in the form of these concrete posts. Older plaques, also usually square, may be fixed on walls either close to the ground or a short distance above.

All these utility posts and plaques can be used as clues, perhaps drawing attention to them by hinting with *When you are blue in the face..., Red faced... and Extremely pale faced... etc.* For example, *What numbers and letters do you see when you are blue in the face?*

And don't forget milestones. Made of either stone or metal, they show the mileage to two towns (one back and the other onward along the road). The top might include the name of the township or parish in which the milestone stands.

Whenever including clues which relate to posts in or other items close to the ground, bear in mind that grass may grow and hide them. It is worth taking a pair of garden shears when you check the route out a day or two before the hunt is due to take place.

Unique Features

There are innumerable features which have been erected over the years, especially during Victorian times and following the two World Wars.

These erections are essentially localised creations, made to commemorate an event, the heroism or patronage of individuals or to provide an amenity for the community.

In addition to war memorials (often listing the names of the local dead), these features can include water fountains, shrines, monuments, pillars, etc. They may include the name of the benefactor and details of the occasion celebrated by the feature.

Also watch for unusual architectural features like pineapples, eagles and lions on gate supports, roofs, etc.

The potential they offer for clues is endless and organisers should be able to devise them without any difficulty.

Miscellaneous items

There are many other potential sources for clues to be found on most routes. Remember that all must be visible from inside the vehicle. Watch out for:

- Drain and manhole covers, especially if they are positioned off the road itself (on a grass verge, for example). Usually made of cast iron, they often include the British Standard kite mark and number (like BS 497), manufacturer details (such as Brickhouse Dudley) as well as other information relating to that particular cover (Grade A, Watergate 450, Ductile S & SH, Ductile Dreadnought, etc.).

- Litter bins may show the manufacturer's name either overtly or tucked away. Lister Bros, of Dursley, Gloucester make litter bins with wooden strips and gaps between them which look a little like waste paper baskets.

- Maximum height and width signs above or near bridges.

- Weather vanes, garden features (gnomes, concrete toadstools, herons, etc.), house, village and street names and small plaques, such as old Insurance devices which often include a policy number. If using features on, in, near or belonging to residential properties, ensure privacy is respected and ask permission of the owners before including them in the hunt.

- Padlocks on gates often show manufacturer (Yale, Chubb, etc.), model and mechanism type. Gates themselves may also provide clues as may horseshoes nailed above doorways and burglar alarm boxes on the sides of properties.

- Grit, salt and other (usually coloured plastic) receptacles may have their contents described in capital letters on the lid and often include a notice stating manufacturer's and other information.

- Building dates on properties may be carved in Roman numerals or normal numbers. Consider converting from one format to the other in your clues.

Directional clues

Organisers may be tempted to include occasional clues within the directional instructions, even though this might not be a particularly good idea.

Some of the more common ploys are as follows:

- **GGT,** an abbreviation which refers to the *Green Grass Triangles* common in some parts of the country where three roads meet. The GGT often contains a signpost.

- **DOFAB,** which means *Drive On For A Bit.* It should only be used where there is a relatively long gap between clues. The next clue should be made fairly obvious so that competitors know when the DOFAB instruction ends.

- **2:30** or **Two Thirty** and similar clues are sometimes used when 30 mph speed limit signs are erected on either side of the road and where a change of route direction follows immediately afterwards, for example *TURN RIGHT AT TWO THIRTY.*

Other advisory road signs may be used with caution, such as hump backed bridge *(TURN LEFT AFTER YOU'VE GOT THE HUMP)* and similar signs.

These examples are by no means comprehensive. Always keep your eyes open for new features and try to vary the nature and complexity of the clues you devise.

Be observant and keep your victims on their toes!

Do not damage the Clues!

Chapter 14

TAKING PART IN A HUNT

So far this book has dealt with treasure hunts from the organiser's point of view. It is now time to examine what the participant (or competitor, or hunter, or victim; call it what you will) should do to have a better chance of winning and obtain maximum enjoyment from the event.

The first thing to do is read and learn about everything the conscientious organiser should have done when actually organising the event.

If the advice in this book has been followed, the participant will understand the restrictions and safety considerations which, in theory at least, will have been taken into account.

Having said that, be aware that the organiser might have overlooked an important aspect and, against all advice, for example, positioned a clue on a dangerous bend.

Participants should do their best to help organisers in every way possible to make their job that much easier. Organising a hunt is not a simple affair and the least anyone can do is be co-operative to reduce the amount of hassle.

Before the event

If your are asked to take part in a hunt, do so willingly. It will be an experience to remember.

If there is an entry fee, pay it without delay and make sure others in your team do likewise; late payment is inconsiderate. Keep the entry ticket(s) safe and note the date and time your team will be expected to arrive at the starting point.

Tell the organiser if there are any special access or dietary considerations (including wheelchair or vegetarian requirements) for you or anyone in your team.

Make sure the vehicle for your team is in roadworthy condition. Also check that it is insured for this type of leisure activity; participants cannot expect the organiser to be liable for loss, damage or injury for problems arising through the neglect of the vehicle owner or driver.

Finally, acquire suitable reference books and maps (see appendices) in case they are needed on the hunt.

Final preparations

Have everything you are likely to need ready in good time before setting off. Your vehicle should have a full tank of petrol and, if you have one, a fully charged mobile telephone in case of emergency.

Items to take with you may be:

- Money, including at least one of each denomination of coinage plus some extra change in case you need to use a public telephone or convenience.
- Reference books and maps of the area likely to be covered by the hunt.
- Clipboard, pad of paper, ball point or felt tip pens and pencils plus a plastic bag or wallet for collecting treasure in case the organiser has forgotten to supply one for each team.
- A torch, compass, weatherproof clothing and/or umbrellas in the event of dark or inclement weather.
- Spare car key. Give it to someone in your team and ask them to carry it on their person in case your own key gets mislaid.
- Your entry (and possibly meal) tickets.
- Anything else you may need.

Do not take animals or children with you unless the organiser has said that it's OK to do so. There may be reasons which make it unwise to bring them.

Depending on the arrangements you have made, assemble your team in the vehicle before going to the starting point or emphasise the need for them to make their own way and to arrive before the time allocated.

During the event

The whole point of the event is for everyone to enjoy themselves. It's only a game, after all. Some people treat these events as though they are a matter of life or death and may upset those around them. Go with an open mind.

Be co-operative and do exactly as the organiser asks. There will be more than enough to occupy his or her mind without you adding to the problems. If your team is asked to start early or asked to wait, don't argue.

Before setting off, all your team should read the rules and make sure they are understood. If in doubt, ask the organiser for clarification. However, do not expect too much help...

Appoint someone to act as leader, preferably not the driver (who needs to concentrate on driving) or the person in the front passenger seat (who will need to act as the main eyes of the team).

Someone familiar with treasure hunt procedures or is very observant should sit in the front passenger seat; it is not necessarily the sole preserve of the driver's spouse. Everyone should look for clues on both sides of the road.

The team leader, armed with the clue sheet, is best employed (in the offside back seat) with reading clues and directions out loud to the others and writing down the answers. The person sitting in the nearside back seat should act as another observer, remembering to look backwards at frequent intervals for hidden clues visible only after being passed.

It can help relieve tension if members of the team change position (and hence responsibilities) in the car at some stage during the proceedings.

The team must avoid conflict and 'told you so' situations. They must respect the driver's decisions when deciding when and where to stop.

The Highway Code and common sense must be used for the safety of everyone in the team as well as other road users, including other participants in the event. Caution is of paramount importance, especially when disembarking from the vehicle.

In the unlikely event that the car is left empty, even for a few moments, while searching for an answer, lock it. Don't take unnecessary chances.

Clue solving is a team activity. Think about what the clue actually says. Is it a transparent clue (one which relates to an obvious item or location) or is it a hidden clue (one where the answer will be found by, perhaps, word association rather than an overt indication)?

Be wary of clues that ask a question. There are still some organisers who put a question mark at the end of a clue when in fact there is no question as such being posed.

On the other hand, clues beginning with the usual asking words (such as how, when, what, who, etc.) indicate that a proper answer to a question is required.

If you are at a total loss with a particular clue, think about what the question might refer to and guess at the answer. All clues should have answers, even if they are pure guesswork. However, make sure that there is only one answer to each clue; the organiser should disregard multiple answers to a clue, even if one happens to be correct.

Hunt clues are very similar and may even be identical to crossword clues. If they have been well conceived, a hint of how to find the answer will be somewhere in the clue.

Do not damage, cover or move any of the clues. To do so is unsporting and childish. All teams must have an equal chance of winning using their intelligence and knowledge.

Selfish acts of vandalism are inexcusable and have no place here. Anyone seen performing them should be reported to the organiser at the earliest opportunity. It helps if you have witnesses from other teams.

However, guile is something different. If another team shows up just as you are about to leave one clue location to proceed to the next, you might like to pretend you are still searching (well away from where you know the answer lies).

Don't forget to look puzzled and shake or scratch your head. You might even like to stand in front of the clue, waving to the other car as it passes by. It's not your fault if they couldn't be bothered to stop.

On the other hand, if you come across another team acting exactly like this, don't even think about whether or not to stop. Park the car as near to them as possible and start searching, making sure you look at every inch of the area, including the ground on which they stand. There may be nothing there, but on the other hand, there might...

It may seem obvious, but don't pass on any of your hard-earned information to other teams. Why should they benefit from your own bloodshed and tears?

If other teams seem to be passing you by with alarming frequency, don't worry. Just because you arrive last at the final venue doesn't necessarily mean that your team will have the lowest score.

If you get lost or there is an emergency of any kind, don't panic. The Panic Envelope will help if you are lost. If there is an emergency, act as you would if the problem had arisen in different circumstances.

Don't be afraid to seek help from another car in the hunt if one happens to appear. By the same token, offer help to other teams if they have an emergency.

At the final venue

When you arrive at the final venue, note your finishing mileage if it is required and check that you have an answer to every clue written in ink (not pencil) on the clue sheet.

Lock the vehicle and take the completed clue sheet, treasure and any other necessary items with you. Hand them to the organiser or his or her helpers and leave them alone to get on with the marking.

Have your meal. Have a drink or two. Relax. Chat to other participants about the experience and relate any amusing or unusual occurrences en route. Keep cool. Don't get drawn into conflict or criticisms. It was only a game, after all.

If you think you might like to organise your own event, observe how the organiser copes and listen to the reactions of other participants.

Finally, get hold of a set of the correct answers and, when your marked clue sheet has been returned to you, compare the two. See where you went wrong and ask the organiser for clarification if there are any uncertainties.

After the event

Thank the organiser personally before leaving to return home, even if your team achieved no more than a dismal last position.

Think about your experience and what others have said about the event. Make your own judgement about any criticisms made, whether in praise or condemnation. Were they justified or could the comments have been coloured by individual team results?

Then consider the event in its entirety. Was the starting point satisfactory or would it have been better if it had been somewhere else?

Was there something inherently wrong with the way the clues had been devised or with the choice of route?

Don't forget to take the facilities at the final venue into account. Were they up to your expectations? Was it suitable? Did it have any shortcomings?

Then organise the next event yourself. Things can only get better with you in charge!

Chapter 15

OTHER HUNT PROVIDERS

If you cannot find anyone to organise a treasure hunt and you are desperate to try one out, there are several businesses and organisations which organise them for the enjoyment of their clients and members. They fall into three general categories.

Vintage or Classic Car Hire Services

Businesses in this category may be able to devise treasure hunts suitable for small groups of people, even for just a couple of folk in a single car.

Usually, these events really are something special and may comprise:

- a chauffeur-driven Vintage, Classic or Antique Limousine car
- gourmet hampers of delicious food and bottles of champagne
- and, of course, a day's treasure hunt.

Some companies provide enhancements to increase enjoyment, e.g. playing gramophones and 1920s/1930s records, visits to places well off the beaten track, old-fashioned games and attendance at special events.

Many of these treasure hunts follow the format where competitors are supplied with an envelope containing the first clue which gives information leading to the next envelope and so on. They may even provide small objects, the use of which is not clear until later in the proceedings when they will be needed to solve a problem.

While taking part, the hunters may be given the opportunity to experience unusual activities, such as visiting places where crafts from yesteryear are still practiced.

These specialist businesses may also arrange accommodation and the supply of period costume to be worn during the event. And the chauffeur is always on hand to ensure the occasion is most enjoyable.

There is no doubt that a treasure hunt organised by one of these firms may well turn out to be one of those remarkably memorable occasions. It will come as no surprise that many of the people who partake of such pleasures are those who wish to celebrate something (such as an anniversary) in a unique way.

The **Antique Limousine Service** at 7 Town Lane, Woodbury, Devon, EX5 1NF (telephone 01395 - 232 - 432) is just one of these specialist businesses whose fame has even spread to television.

One of their hunts was designed for eight people. The object of the hunt was to find an empty croquet box and fill it with all the items needed to play a game – and play! One envelope was even delivered by a live tortoise!

The men rode penny-farthing bicycles and the ladies took a short ferry ride. All were treated to a superb gourmet picnic with champagne in castle grounds and a Devonshire Cream Tea. Everyone was presented with a special memento.

To see if there are suitable companies in your area, check out the local press, Yellow Pages, Business Pages and similar directories or internet-based business search facilities. 'Car Hire - Chauffeur Driven' and 'Entertainment Agencies' listings are a good place to start. Even travel agencies and Information Centres may be able to help.

Corporate Entertainment Services

Other businesses devise bespoke treasure hunts (among other things) for larger companies who use them for team building and managerial problem solving exercises away from the office environment.

The format of these hunts varies according to the expertise and experience of individual suppliers as well as what they hope to achieve and the number of clients taking part.

Check out Yellow Pages, Business Pages and similar directories or internet-based business search facilities. Try looking under 'Corporate Entertainment', 'Entertainment', 'Event Organisers' and 'Promotion Consultants'.

Motor Clubs and Associations

In addition to the above types of business, it might be worthwhile joining a local or regional Motor Club.

Many are listed in the MSA Fixtures and Motor Sports Clubs Book, which is updated annually. These clubs run all sorts of motoring competitions, including treasure hunts.

Others may provide members with magazines and newsletters: there is always the possibility that localised hunts are advertised in them. The Civil Service Motoring Association, for example, produces the 'Motoring and Leisure' magazine.

You could look in Yellow Pages under 'Clubs and Associations' and 'Sports Clubs and Associations' having a motoring bias.

Colleagues, friends and family may also be able to point you in the right direction.

Journey's end

APPENDICES

A: Reference Material

- This handbook
- The Highway Code
- Ordnance Survey Landranger maps
- A good Dictionary (e.g. Chambers English), complete with abbreviations, foreign phrases, etc.
- Books on woodland/wild flowers and herbs
- A good Encyclopædia
- Localised Travel and Tourist guidebooks
- Books and pamphlets associated with any organisation for which the event is being organised and from which pertinent clues may be devised.

Add your own useful references here:

....
....
....
....
....
....
....
....
....
....
....
....
....
....
....
....
....
....

B: The Countryside Code

- Enjoy the countryside and respect its life and work
- Guard against all risk of fire
- Fasten all gates
- Keep your dogs under close control
- Keep to public paths across farmland
- Use gates and stiles to cross fences, hedges and walls
- Leave livestock, crops and machinery alone
- Take your litter home
- Help to keep all water clean
- Protect wildlife, plants and trees
- Take special care on country roads
- Make no unnecessary noise.

C: Examples of Treasures

This list shows some of the items (and suggested clues) which competitors could reasonably be expected to gather during a hunt. Bear in mind that some may only be available at certain times of the year.

Natural items

Item	**Possible Clue**
ACORN	Origin of large oaks
BURDOCK LEAF	Antidote for a sting; Dandelion's mixer
BUTTERCUP	Daisy's mate
CATKIN	Pussy's relation
CLOVER LEAF	Luck of the Irish?
DAISY	Buttercup's associate; A natural chain maker
DANDELION	Jungle King in fashionable clothing Nature's timepiece; Lion's teeth A Taraxacum Officinale
FEATHER	Bird's clothing; Flighty pen
FOXGLOVE	Vixen's mitten; Fairy thimbles
GRASS	Don't let it grow under your feet; This sounds like it can be smoked by druggies; Something that is always greener on the other side
HOLLY	Ivy's seasonal friend; Prickly Christmas evergreen
IVY	Roman number for creeping
NETTLE	Natural green stinger
OAK LEAF	Cover from the Pride of England
POPPY	Source of opium; Haig's reminder; Start of Thomas de Quincey's bad habit
POTATO	Veggie stencil maker; Walter Raleigh's ingredient; A chip maker; Crisp source
THISTLE	A prickly Scot

PINE CONE	Tree-borne weather forecaster
WHITE PEBBLE	Un caillou blanc
WILLOW LEAF	Natural covering for a cricket bat
PIECE OF WOOD	Toucher for good luck
WOOL (SHEEP'S YARN)	Wolf's under cover disguise; Old tale told by lamb's parents

Unnatural items

BEER MAT or COASTER	Pedestal for drinker
BOTTLE or JAR (empty)	Glass container devoid of contents
BOTTLE or JAR (full)	Glass receptacle complete with contents
BUS TICKET	Permit for an omnibus
CAN (full)	Sealed cylinder with internal beverage
COIN	Loose tool for payment
COMB	A row of teeth; a plastic groomer
LEAFLET	Information foldup
MATCH BOX	Container for fiery timber; Holder v Striking
NEWSPAPER	Tabloid or Broadsheet; Daily doings informer
OTHER BRITISH COINS (pre-Euro)	Monarch's head
1 PENCE COIN	Castle entrance safety measure; Cash with a grill, but not for cooking
2 PENCE COIN	Plume for bartering
5 PENCE COIN	Crowned Flower of Scotland
10 PENCE COIN	Sterling lion
20 PENCE COIN	A Rose and Crown; A heptagon
50 PENCE COIN	A heptagon (also a 20p coin)
£1 COIN (depending on type)	Leek; lion and a unicorn, etc.
£2 COIN	Payment device with two-tone concentric circles
PLATFORM TICKET	Allows you to wait, not ride
POSTCARD	Pictorial rectangle for despatch

D: Quiz Questions

Should you decide to include a quiz in your hunt, here are some sample questions which could be included. All are loosely associated with treasure in one way or another.

Question	**Answer**
In Tolkien's *The Hobbit,* who calls the Ring his 'Precious'?	Gollum
In Tolkien's *The Hobbit,* who stole the Ring?	Bilbo Baggins
Who wrote *Treasure Island?*	Robert Louis Stevenson
What was the name of the ship in *Treasure Island?*	The Hispaniola
Who is the captain of the ship in *Treasure Island?*	Captain Trelawney
Who is the cabin boy in *Treasure Island?*	Jim Hawkins
In *Treasure Island,* what food does Ben Gunn yearn for?	Cheese
In *Treasure Island,* what is Captain Flint's catch phrase?	Pieces of Eight
Who wrote *King Solomon's Mines?*	H Rider Haggard
Which Book of the Old Testament tells of the Israelites making a Golden Calf, much to Moses annoyance?	Exodus
Which children's author wrote *The Treasure Hunters?*	Enid Blyton
Who wrote *The Treasure Seekers?*	E Nesbitt
Which precious metal worker wrote *She Stoops to Conquer?*	Oliver Goldsmith
How many are on the Treasure Island in the title of Enid Blyton's Book?	Five
What is the elemental name for Quicksilver?	Mercury (Hg)
What sport is played on a diamond?	Baseball

If you were born into wealth, what sort of cutlery might you have in your mouth? A silver spoon

What is the chemical symbol for:
Gold? Au
Silver? Ag
Diamond? C (Carbon)

Who sang the title song for the James Bond film *Diamonds are Forever?* Shirley Bassey

Who played the part of Tiffany Case in *Diamonds are Forever?* Jill St John

Which actress had an overdose of body paint in the James Bond film *Goldfinger?* Shirley Eaton

Who played Auric Goldfinger in *Goldfinger?* Gert Fröbe

Who played Bond in *The Man with the Golden Gun?* Roger Moore

Which actor played the part of *The Man with the Golden Gun?* Christopher Lee

Which character did Christopher Lee play in *The Man with the Golden Gun?* Scaramanga

Who played Bond in *Goldeneye?* Pierce Brosnan

Which actor starred silently in *The Gold Rush?* Charlie Chaplin

In which 1960 film does the richest woman in the world fall in love with a poor Indian doctor? The Millionairess

Who sings *Goodness, gracious me* in *The Millionairess?* Sophia Loren and Peter Sellers

Who wrote *The Billion Dollar Brain?* Len Deighton

Not many people know which British actor starred in the 1967 film *Billion Dollar Brain.* Who was he? Michael Caine

In which year did the Great Train Robbery occur? 1963

Which 1980 film starred David Essex as a racing motorcyclist killed at the peak of his success? Silver Dream Racer

Name the acting father and daughter who starred in the film *On Golden Pond.* Henry and Jane Fonda

Name the 1981 film in which a father and daughter (both on and off the screen) become reconciled.	On Golden Pond
Which group originally released the song *Lucy in the Sky with Diamonds?*	The Beatles
Who sang *Lucy in the Sky with Diamonds* in 1975?	Elton John
Who sang *Band of Gold* in 1970?	Freda Payne
Who sang *Pearl's a Singer* in 1977?	Elkie Brookes
The Golden Gate Bridge is at which city?	San Francisco
Which American state is called the:	
Silver State?	Nevada
Golden State?	California
Diamond State?	Delaware
Where does America keep its gold bullion reserves?	Fort Knox
Which precious mineral or gem is associated with:	
25th Wedding Anniversaries?	Silver
40th Wedding Anniversaries?	Ruby
60th Wedding Anniversaries?	Diamond
Who released the song *Silver Lady* in 1977?	David Soul
Whose tomb was discovered in 1924 by Howard Carter?	Tutankhamun
Where is Tutankhamen's treasure to be found?	In the museum at Cairo
In which 1948 film did three gold prospectors come to grief through greed?	Treasure of the Sierra Madre
What is the rarest diamond colour?	Blood Red
What was the name of the largest diamond ever found?	Cullinan
What is Golden Saxifrage?	A plant *(Chrysoplenium)*
What is Golden Rod?	A plant *(Solidago)*
What sort of animal is a Silverback?	Gorilla
Sergeant Bilko was played by whom?	Phil Silvers

Who shouted 'Hi ho, Silver'? — The Lone Ranger

Which actor played Tonto? — Jay Silverheels

What did The Lone Ranger fire from his pistol? — Silver bullets

What form of transport was The Silver Arrow? — A train (A boat train)

What was the name of Francis Drake's ship, as depicted on old halfpenny coins? — The Golden Hind

What is every cloud supposed to have? — A silver lining

What does El Dorado mean? — The Golden Land (or City)

When the Emperor Caligula forgot to order boats for his intended invasion of Britain, he commanded his troops to steal treasure from Neptune, the god of the Sea, by way of revenge. What was that treasure? — Sea shells

Who blesses a rose made of wrought gold on the fourth Sunday in Lent? — The Pope

What is a Goldspink? — A bird (Goldfinch)

What type of bird laid golden eggs? — Goose

Which ancient Greek plucked a golden bough before he entered the Underworld? — Aeneas

What was the name of the ram's coat sought by the Argonauts? — The Golden Fleece

What is the common name for *Betula Pendula?* — Silver Birch tree

What is Black Diamond? — Coal

What could the Philosopher's Stone do? — Turn base metals into gold

Where would you look at a silver screen? — In a cinema

What metal is silver paper made from? — Aluminium

Which Phrygian king's touch turned everything to gold? — Midas

In which year did the Californian Gold Rush begin? — 1848

What bodily feature might show silver threads amongst the gold? — Hair

E: Element Table in Symbol Order

Symbol	Name	Number
Ac	Actinium	89
Ag	Silver	47
Al	Aluminium	13
Am	Americum	95
Ar	Argon	18
As	Arsenic	33
At	Astatine	85
Au	Gold	79
B	Boron	5
Ba	Barium	56
Be	Beryllium	4
Bi	Bismuth	83
Bk	Berkelium	97
Br	Bromine	35
C	Carbon	6
Ca	Calcium	20
Cd	Cadmium	48
Ce	Cerium	58
Cf	Californium	98
Cl	Chlorine	17
Cm	Curium	96
Co	Cobalt	27
Cr	Chromium	24
Cs	Cesium	55
Cu	Copper	29
Dy	Dysprosium	66
Er	Erbium	68
Es	Einsteinium	99
Eu	Europium	63
F	Fluorine	9
Fe	Iron	26
Fm	Fermium	100
Fr	Francium	87
Ga	Gallium	31
Gd	Gadolinium	64
Ge	Germanium	32
H	Hydrogen	1
Ha	Hahnium	105
He	Helium	2
Hf	Hafnium	72
Hg	Mercury	80
Ho	Holmium	67
I	Iodine	53
In	Indium	49
Ir	Iridium	77
K	Potassium	19
Kr	Krypton	36
Ku	Kurchatovium	104
La	Lanthanum	57
Li	Lithium	3
Lr	Lawrencium	103
Lu	Lutetium	71
Md	Mendelevium	101
Mg	Magnesium	12
Mn	Manganese	25
Mo	Molybdenum	42
N	Nitrogen	7
Na	Sodium	11
Nb	Niobium	41
Nd	Neodymium	60
Ne	Neon	10
Ni	Nickel	28
No	Nobelium	102
Np	Neptunium	93
O	Oxygen	8
Os	Osmium	76
P	Phosphorus	15
Pa	Protactinium	91
Pb	Lead	82
Pd	Palladium	46
Pm	Promethium	61
Po	Polonium	84
Pr	Praseodymium	59
Pt	Platinum	78
Pu	Plutonium	94
Ra	Radium	88
Rb	Rubidium	37
Re	Rhenium	75
Rh	Rhodium	45
Rn	Radon	86
Ru	Ruthenium	44
S	Sulphur	16
Sb	Antimony	51
Sc	Scandium	21
Se	Selenium	34
Si	Silicon	14
Sm	Samarium	62
Sn	Tin	50
Sr	Strontium	38
Ta	Tantalum	73
Tb	Terbium	65
Tc	Technetium	43
Te	Tellurium	52
Th	Thorium	90
Ti	Titanium	22
Tl	Thallium	81
Tm	Thulium	69
U	Uranium	92
V	Vanadium	23
W	Tungsten	74
Xe	Xenon	54
Y	Yttrium	39
Yb	Ytterbium	70
Zn	Zinc	30
Zr	Zirconium	40

F: Element Table in Name Order

Name	Symbol	Number
Actinium	Ac	89
Aluminium	A	113
Americum	Am	95
Antimony	Sb	51
Argon	Ar	18
Arsenic	As	33
Astatine	At	85
Barium	Ba	56
Berkelium	Bk	97
Beryllium	Be	4
Bismuth	Bi	83
Boron	B	5
Bromine	Br	35
Cadmium	Cd	48
Calcium	Ca	20
Californium	Cf	98
Carbon	C	6
Cerium	Ce	58
Cesium	Cs	55
Chlorine	Cl	17
Chromium	Cr	24
Cobalt	Co	27
Copper	Cu	29
Curium	Cm	96
Dysprosium	Dy	66
Einsteinium	Es	99
Erbium	Er	68
Europium	Eu	63
Fermium	Fm	100
Fluorine	F	9
Francium	Fr	87
Gadolinium	Gd	64
Gallium	Ga	31
Germanium	Ge	32
Gold	Au	79
Hafnium	Hf	72
Hahnium	Ha	105
Helium	He	2
Holmium	Ho	67
Hydrogen	H	1
Indium	In	49
Iodine	I	53
Iridium	Ir	77
Iron	Fe	26
Krypton	Kr	36
Kurchatovium	Ku	104
Lanthanum	La	57
Lawrencium	Lr	103
Lead	Pb	82
Lithium	Li	3
Lutetium	Lu	71
Magnesium	Mg	12
Manganese	Mn	25
Mendelevium	Md	101
Mercury	Hg	80
Molybdenum	Mo	42
Neodymium	Nd	60
Neon	Ne	10
Neptunium	Np	93
Nickel	Ni	28
Niobium	Nb	41
Nitrogen	N	7
Nobelium	No	102
Osmium	Os	76
Oxygen	O	8
Palladium	Pd	46
Phosphorus	P	15
Platinum	Pt	78
Plutonium	Pu	94
Polonium	Po	84
Potassium	K	19
Praseodymium	Pr	59
Promethium	Pm	61
Protactinium	Pa	91
Radium	Ra	88
Radon	Rn	86
Rhenium	Re	75
Rhodium	Rh	45
Rubidium	Rb	37
Ruthenium	Ru	44
Samarium	Sm	62
Scandium	Sc	21
Selenium	Se	34
Silicon	Si	14
Silver	Ag	47
Sodium	Na	11
Strontium	Sr	38
Sulphur	S	16
Tantalum	Ta	73
Technetium	Tc	43
Tellurium	Te	52
Terbium	Tb	65
Thallium	Tl	81
Thorium	Th	90
Thulium	Tm	69
Tin	Sn	50
Titanium	Ti	22
Tungsten	W	74
Uranium	U	92
Vanadium	V	23
Xenon	Xe	54
Ytterbium	Yb	70
Yttrium	Y	39
Zinc	Zn	30
Zirconium	Zr	40

G: Element Table in Number Order

Number	Symbol	Name
1	H	Hydrogen
2	He	Helium
3	Li	Lithium
4	Be	Beryllium
5	B	Boron
6	C	Carbon
7	N	Nitrogen
8	O	Oxygen
9	F	Fluorine
10	Ne	Neon
11	Na	Sodium
12	Mg	Magnesium
13	Al	Aluminium
14	Si	Silicon
15	P	Phosphorus
16	S	Sulphur
17	Cl	Chlorine
18	Ar	Argon
19	K	Potassium
20	Ca	Calcium
21	Sc	Scandium
22	Ti	Titanium
23	V	Vanadium
24	Cr	Chromium
25	Mn	Manganese
26	Fe	Iron
27	Co	Cobalt
28	Ni	Nickel
29	Cu	Copper
30	Zn	Zinc
31	Ga	Gallium
32	Ge	Germanium
33	As	Arsenic
34	Se	Selenium
35	Br	Bromine
36	Kr	Krypton
37	Rb	Rubidium
38	Sr	Strontium
39	Y	Yttrium
40	Zr	Zirconium
41	Nb	Niobium
42	Mo	Molybdenum
43	Tc	Technetium
44	Ru	Ruthenium
45	Rh	Rhodium
46	Pd	Palladium
47	Ag	Silver
48	Cd	Cadmium
49	In	Indium
50	Sn	Tin
51	Sb	Antimony
52	Te	Tellurium
53	I	Iodine
54	Xe	Xenon
55	Cs	Cesium
56	Ba	Barium
57	La	Lanthanum
58	Ce	Cerium
59	Pr	Praseodymium
60	Nd	Neodymium
61	Pm	Promethium
62	Sm	Samarium
63	Eu	Europium
64	Gd	Gadolinium
65	Tb	Terbium
66	Dy	Dysprosium
67	Ho	Holmium
68	Er	Erbium
69	Tm	Thulium
70	Yb	Ytterbium
71	Lu	Lutetium
72	Hf	Hafnium
73	Ta	Tantalum
74	W	Tungsten
75	Re	Rhenium
76	Os	Osmium
77	Ir	Iridium
78	Pt	Platinum
79	Au	Gold
80	Hg	Mercury
81	Tl	Thallium
82	Pb	Lead
83	Bi	Bismuth
84	Po	Polonium
85	At	Astatine
86	Rn	Radon
87	Fr	Francium
88	Ra	Radium
89	Ac	Actinium
90	Th	Thorium
91	Pa	Protactinium
92	U	Uranium
93	Np	Neptunium
94	Pu	Plutonium
95	Am	Americum
96	Cm	Curium
97	Bk	Berkelium
98	Cf	Californium
99	Es	Einsteinium
100	Fm	Fermium
101	Md	Mendelevium
102	No	Nobelium
103	Lr	Lawrencium
104	Ku	Kurchatovium
105	Ha	Hahnium

H: Alphabets and Numerals

BINARY DIGIT ALPHABET		MORSE CODE ALPHABET		ROMAN NUMERALS			
Code	Letter	Code	Letter	Code	Letter		
00001	A	. –	A	I	1	XLI	41
00010	B	– . . .	B	II	2	L	50
00011	C	– . – .	C	III	3	LI	51
00100	D	– . .	D	IV	4	LX	60
00101	E	.	E	V	5	LXI	61
00110	F	. – .	F	VI	6	LXX	70
00111	G	– – .	G	VII	7	LXXI	71
01000	H	. . . .	H	VIII	8	LXXX	80
01001	I	. .	I	IX	9	LXXXI	81
01010	J	. – – –	J	X	10	XC	90
01011	K	– . –	K	XI	11	XCI	91
01100	L	. – . .	L	XII	12	C	100
01101	M	– –	M	XIII	13	CC	200
01110	N	– .	N	XIV	14	CCC	300
01111	O	– – –	O	XV	15	CD	400
10000	P	. – – .	P	XVI	16	D	500
10001	Q	– – . –	Q	XVII	17	DC	600
10010	R	. – .	R	XVIII	18	DCC	700
10011	S	. . .	S	XIX	19	DCCC	800
10100	T	–	T	XX	20	CM	900
10101	U	. . . –	U	XXI	21	M	1000
10110	V	. . . –	V	XXII	22	MD	1500
10111	W	. – –	W	XXIII	23	MCM	1900
11000	X	– . . –	X	XXIV	24	MM	2000
11001	Y	– . – –	Y	XXV	25		
11010	Z	– – . .	Z	XXVI	26		
		. . – – . .	?	XXVII	27		
		. – . – . –	stop	XXVIII	28		
				XXIX	29		
				XXX	30		
				XXXI	31		
				XL	40		

Examples of Dates

MCDXCII
= 1492.

MDCCCLXVIII
= 1868.

MCMXLV
= 1945.

EXAMPLE		YOUR CODE		YOUR CODE		YOUR CODE	
Real Letter	Replace With	Real Letter	Replace With	Real Letter	Replace With	Real Letter	Replace With
A	N	A	____	A	____	A	____
B	O	B	____	B	____	B	____
C	P	C	____	C	____	C	____
D	Q	D	____	D	____	D	____
E	R	E	____	E	____	E	____
F	S	F	____	F	____	F	____
G	T	G	____	G	____	G	____
H	U	H	____	H	____	H	____
I	V	I	____	I	____	I	____
J	W	J	____	J	____	J	____
K	X	K	____	K	____	K	____
L	Y	L	____	L	____	L	____
M	Z	M	____	M	____	M	____
N	A	N	____	N	____	N	____
O	B	O	____	O	____	O	____
P	C	P	____	P	____	P	____
Q	D	Q	____	Q	____	Q	____
R	E	R	____	R	____	R	____
S	F	S	____	S	____	S	____
T	G	T	____	T	____	T	____
U	H	U	____	U	____	U	____
V	I	V	____	V	____	V	____
W	J	W	____	W	____	W	____
X	K	X	____	X	____	X	____
Y	L	Y	____	Y	____	Y	____
Z	M	Z	____	Z	____	Z	____

Hunt Starter Packs

Especially for readers of this book

The author has produced two Starter Packs to help you save time when organising your own Treasure Hunt. Each pack contains basic stationery with spaces for you to enter information specific to your event.

Please note that they are not suitable for organising Mystery Drives.

Pack One - Standard Treasure Hunts
Comprising one A3 and one A4 poster; 13 copies of a Standard Treasure Hunt instructions covering page; 48 entry tickets and one Participants List. Complete with instructions on how to fill in the spaces.

Pack Two - Scatter Treasure Hunts
Comprising one A3 and one A4 poster; 13 copies of a Scatter Treasure Hunt instructions covering page; 48 entry tickets and one Participants List. Complete with instructions on how to fill in the spaces.

Please photocopy the order form on page 124 rather than damage the book.

Hunt Starter Pack Order Form

Item	Price each	Quantity	Amount due
Starter Pack One Standard Treasure Hunt	£6.00		
Starter Pack Two Scatter Treasure Hunt	£6.00		
How to Organise (and Win!) Car Treasure Hunts	£7.95		
Total amount due:			

Please enter your details (in CAPITALS):

Name: ....

Address: ....

....

....

Post code: ....

Telephone: ....

Send this completed form to:
Allan Frost
1 Buttermere Drive, Priorslee, Telford, Shropshire, TF2 9RE.

Cheques should be made payable to Allan Frost.
Offer applies to addresses in the United Kingdom only.
Prices include postage and packing.
Allow up to 28 days for delivery.

Personal Notes